A HISTORY OF IDEAS

A History of Ideas

Kevin O'Donnell

LION
ACCESS
GUIDES

Published by
Lion Publishing plc
Mayfield House, 256 Banbury Road,
Oxford OX2 7DH, England
www.lion-publishing.co.uk
ISBN 0 7459 5091 4

First edition 2003
10 9 8 7 6 5 4 3 2 1 0

All rights reserved

A catalogue record for this book is
available from the British Library

Typeset in 10.25/11 Venetian 301
Printed and bound in China

Text acknowledgments
Scripture quotations taken from the
Holy Bible, New International Version, copyright
© 1973, 1978, 1984 International Bible
Society. Used by permission of Zondervan
and Hodder & Stoughton Limited.
All rights reserved. The 'NIV' and
'New International Version' trademarks
are registered in the United States Patent
and Trademark Office by International
Bible Society. Use of either trademark
requires the permission of International
Bible Society. UK trademark number
1448790.
Excerpts from the Qur'an are taken from
The Holy Qur'an, translated by Abdullah
Yusuf Ali, Wordsworth Editions Ltd,
2000.

Picture acknowledgments
Please see page 160.

Contents

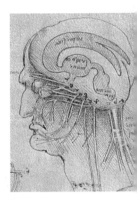

Note
Throughout this series the convention is followed of dating events by the abbreviations BCE (Before Common Era) and CE (Common Era). They correspond precisely to the more familiar BC and AD.

Introducing a History of Ideas

It has been suggested that the long span of millennia extending from the dawn of time until today can be compared to a human being with arms outstretched. If we imagine that the tip of the longest finger on the left hand is the beginning of the cosmos, then the fingernail on the longest finger of the right hand is the last 100,000 years or so, when *Homo sapiens* have been in existence. Today is the very edge of that nail. All that space in-between, running along the arms and over the shoulders, represents millions of years. It is a staggering length of time, and most of it has been devoid of human life. This should make us very, very humble.

Homo sapiens were so called because of our 'wisdom', our advanced brains and language, which enable us to think and to reason things out. In human beings, the universe became conscious of itself.

Ideas are powerful, but ethereal and abstract things. Early in Fyodor Dostoevsky's *Crime and*

Punishment, the young man, Raskolnikov, is found lounging about in his room. The maid only enters occasionally to tidy things up; it is a poverty-stricken 'bachelor pad'. She asks Raskolnikov what he is doing. He replies that he is working. In response to her incredulous stare, he explains that he has been thinking. She laughs. Yet our ability to think sets us apart from other animals. Thinking is a form of work, and the ideas that people have had through the ages have changed the way we live. Ideas are powerful tools. The history of philosophy, 'the love of wisdom', is about thinking clearly. It has embraced three basic questions from the beginning of human civilization:

◆ What is the universe made of?
◆ What is the meaning of life?
◆ How should we live?

This book follows the history of ideas through from ancient times to the present day, and blends philosophy, religion, ethical and spiritual concerns. Where necessary, background information has been supplied, for example with regard to some of the world faiths. As with other books in this series, there is a Rapid Factfinder at the end to help if you want to look something up quickly.

The Thinker by
Auguste Rodin
(1840–1917).

IN THE BEGINNING…
MYTH

The earliest evidence of intellectual advance and creativity in hominids was found at Olduvai Gorge in Eastern Africa. Here, Homo habilis made simple, stone tools about 2.5 million years ago. There was little development until about 40,000 years ago. Then there was a sudden leap, a widespread artistic flourish across the inhabited world: elaborate carvings, figurines and cave paintings appeared. It was a great cultural surge forwards.

The most recent discovery of cave paintings took place in 1994 at

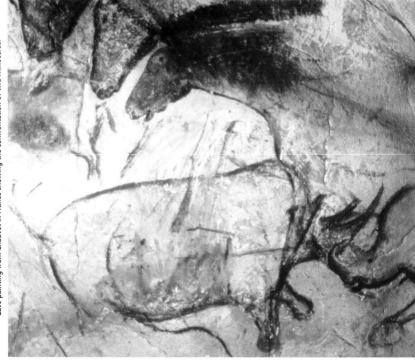

Cave painting from Chauvet in France showing the confrontation of two rhinoceros.

Chauvet in France. In a cavern entered by a shaft, three potholers discovered paintings of a mammoth, lions, panthers, buffalo and rhinoceros. One of the potholers declared, 'We had a date with prehistory that day.' Until this discovery, it had been thought that cave paintings had gradually improved from about 25,000 years ago. The Chauvet paintings were dated at about 31,000–33,000 years ago; the skill was advanced.

Why were these paintings made? The French scholar Henri Breuil first suggested that cave paintings were a form of magic to give the hunters power over the animals, or even protection from them. Recent theories have pointed out that there were large amounts of footprints in the caves near the paintings. They may have been places of initiation.

Paintings and carvings show an ability to make symbols and to begin conceptual thought. The external world was organized and analysed, and people tried to impose order and meaning upon it. It was vivid, visual and evolved into myth.

Contents

The eyes and hands of the first painters and engravers were as fine as any that came later. There was a grace from the start.

ART CRITIC JOHN BERGER, SPEAKING OF THE CAVE PAINTINGS AT CHAUVET

Time to Think

As humans settled down into farming communities, they had more time and energy to think and to wonder. Myth and ritual developed apace, as did the gift of writing.

The earliest evidence of a settled village, where people farmed rather than hunted, is at Shanidar in Iraq. This dates from about 8,000 BCE. The transition from hunting to farming – the neolithic revolution – brought about a paradigm shift in human development, social organization and understanding. Herding animals and cultivating crops brought people into settlements and allowed more time for reflection and creativity. Life was not just about a struggle for survival, foraging and hunting at great personal risk. Clans settled and intermarried, forging links and associations for their mutual benefit.

Early thinkers sought to map out their world so they could control it and navigate their way through it. The movement of the sun and the moon in the heavens was discovered to be regular, and the coming and going of the seasons could be predicted – invaluable for early farmers who then knew when to sow and when to harvest. These astral entities

The primitive mentality does not invent myths, it experiences them.

G.S. KIRK,
MYTH: ITS MEANING AND FUNCTIONS IN ANCIENT AND OTHER CULTURES

were numinous things, mysteries that moved, and were thus alive. Why else would things have motion and such power and influence? They were gods.

Magic and the shaman

The first philosophers were in tune with the spirits; the shaman danced the first principles of the cosmos. The Unseen was all around, interweaving with this world, the forces behind fire and water, the wind and the fertility of the land. The ancestors joined with those spirits. We do not know the precise delineations of their early beliefs until things began to be written down many years later. There are hints and clues only, scraps surviving in later myths and described rituals, and glimpses in archaeology, such as the curled-up skeleton of a Neanderthal man covered

Beauty and awe stir up imaginative and creative faculties in human beings.

with red dye and a circle of flowers in an ancient burial site in Shanidar.

People had begun to look up and around and to wonder. To wonder is to begin to understand.

sky. Today, by contrast, some rip the personal dimension out of the world altogether: to materialistic scientists, it is all mechanics. Can a human person just be reduced to atoms and chemicals? Others

The irreducible symbol

It is easy to dismiss ancient myths and ritual systems as primitive, a childish grasp of the universe. That is true in part, but these ideas were symbol systems, and we cannot dispense with the symbolic even in modern hi-tech science. They were the first attempts to analyse the world and to ask the interconnected questions of 'Why?' and 'How?' For the ancients, water flowed because of a spirit's will; the sun moved because a god sailed across the

wonder if there can be room for mechanisms and meanings at a deeper level. Perhaps the 'why' is different from the 'how'. Curiously, history shows us that the scientific quest and the spiritual journey began simultaneously as two halves of the same coin — wonder at how things worked, and awe about why anything should be at all.

Dancers and Dreamers

The figure of the shaman survives among some tribal groups, such as the American Indians, and the Aborigines give us an insight into continuing, 'living' myths with the Dreamtime.

The early priests/scientists, the 'go-betweens', were the shamans. Tribal culture had the wise man, the initiate who claimed to be able to communicate with the gods. They said that they received messages, could let their spirits slip out of their bodies, and take the form of animals, such as eagles. Their rituals involved going into a trance when beating a drum decorated with sacred symbols. They knew the lore of plants and herbal remedies, acting as healers, and they danced and sang the stories of the gods.

These ancient ways have been passed on to modern individuals in tribal groups such as the American Indians. They have the sacred dance, words to enchant, elaborate skills to paint sand pictures that are supposed to link earth with the spirits, and the sweat lodge. The sweat lodge is an enclosed space that has hot stones and steam. This is supposed to purify body and soul, and brings about a trance-enhancing state.

Nourlangie Lightning Man, an Aboriginal rock painting of a Dreamtime deity, Arnhem Land, Australia.

A modern-day shaman wearing clothes made from animal skins.

Traditional cultures are close to the rhythms of nature, and have often preserved their herbal lore. Anita Roddick, the founder of the Body Shop, has travelled around the world to seek out this arcane knowledge of natural ingredients to use in cleansing and relaxing agents.

The dream was and is important to them. Here, they would take their spirit journeys, converse with ancestors, and meet their spirit guardian in an animal form. Dreams were holy ground. Their techniques used meditation and visualization to encourage visions and the hearing of messages from the depths of their minds.

Abiding wisdom

These rituals and concepts might be alien to contemporary readers, but tribal groups can often preserve insights and values that Western society has forgotten. The Unseen cannot be observed under a microscope or measured. Love, mercy, joy and value are not concrete realities. We cannot drain away all the invisibles. Things that cannot be seen or experienced by any of the five, physical senses can still be felt and intuited and become tangible in our lives.

THE DREAMTIME

The Australian Aborigines speak of the Dreamtime, which began before the creation of the universe, extending back to the primordial mists of eternity. They have a rich mythology, populated by gods and supernatural beings, such as the Rainbow Serpent, the Lightning Men and the Wagilag Sisters. These beings travelled across the unmade world and gave it form. The Dreamtime is not only a distant creation myth, but a pattern, a set of spiritual/moral laws for life itself.

There are several different Dreamings across the land, sometimes connected to a rock or a natural feature, while others stretch for miles. There are special rituals and ceremonies for maintaining the link with the Dreaming. The Dreamtime is not illusion and unreality ('it's just a dream'), but the reality behind material reality.

Dying and Rising

There are common symbols and stories in myths across the ages and across different cultures. They speak of deep drives and needs within the human psyche. One prevalent symbol is sacrifice: the dying/rising god.

The English scholar Sir James Frazer (1854–1941), of Cambridge University, wrote about types of myths in *The Golden Bough*, first published in 1922. He was particularly interested in the idea of sympathetic magic, whereby an action, a ritual, an offering or a death would be seen to affect the external world and the course of nature. His studies centred upon nature myths and ideas of the 'corn king', the dying and rising god who represented the forces of nature.

When autumn and winter came, the god 'died', journeying to the underworld. He rose again in spring. These nature deities went under different names in different places: Balder among the Norsemen, Osiris among the Egyptians, Mithras among the

> *As in the woods in winter cold the mistletoe… such seemed upon the shady holm-oak the leafy gold, so rustled in the gentle breeze the golden leaf.*
> VIRGIL, *THE AENEID*

BALDER THE BRAVE

Balder was the second son of Odin in the Norse myths. He was troubled by dreams of his coming death.

He told his mother, the goddess Frigg, who asked all the gods and all things to swear an oath that they would never harm Balder — earth, wood, stone, sickness, the animals… everything but one little shoot of mistletoe.

The gods liked to sport and they threw things at Balder, laughing as a sword would not hurt him, and rocks bounced off. Loki, the god of evil, disguised himself as an old woman and heard about the mistletoe. He took a shoot and handed it to a blind god, tricking him into throwing it as a dart at Balder. It pierced the god and he dropped down dead. The gods were speechless and Balder's spirit went down to the Underworld. It was agreed that only if every living creature wept tears for Balder would he return to life. They did, except an old woman in a cave, assumed to be Loki.

Persians, and Dionysus among the Greeks. The force of nature was sometimes envisaged as feminine, and earth mothers would descend into the earth too, such as the ancient Babylonian deity Tammuz.

One form of sympathetic up, by recycling. Life is vicarious, involving a constant sacrifice. The sun burns itself out, creatures are born, others die to make room for them. The old myths can be cast aside as childish and primitive, but, seen from another angle, they

In the myth of the corn king, the god dies in winter, then rises again in the spring.

magic involved the king who was to be killed in imitation of the god: the king's blood ensured the ripening of the corn. Frazer argued that this took place in a sacred grove at the site of a mistletoe tree, considered particularly sacred in ancient times. This blossom was the 'golden bough' as the Roman poet Virgil suggested.

Sacrifice and nature
We live in an ecosystem that works by life and death, by a constant birthing and giving

contain deep insights into the dynamics of reality. The theme of weeping for the god is common in these fertility myths, and the tears, or the love of one special person, usually bring them back.

Out of Chaos

Myths often concern themselves with beginnings and the creation of worlds. The stories and details of how the world was made differ among ancient peoples, but there are some common, underlying themes.

Chaos is tamed – the forces of chaos, of formlessness, emptiness and destruction, are conquered by a god or the gods. These forces are usually personified as a monster, a dragon or a beast such as a raging bull. The world is made from the body of the chaos beast, and its blood gives life. Human beings are made as the servants or slaves of the gods.

Marduk and Tiamat

From the Ancient Near East comes the story of a fierce battle between a god and chaos. The version preserved on stone tablets at ancient Babylon told the story of Marduk and Tiamat: the *Enuma Elish*. Tiamat was the chaos beast, a dragon that symbolized the abyss. This was a mythical void of darkness and raging waters before anything else existed. Some of the ancients thought that water surrounded the earth (which was flat) and not empty space. They looked around and saw blue skies; water fell from up above in the form of rain.

[Marduk] rested, and inspected her [Tiamat's] corpse.
He divided the monstrous shape and created marvels [from it].
He sliced her in half like a fish for drying:
Half of her he put up to roof the sky,
Drew a bolt across and made a guard hold it.
Her waters he arranged so that they could not escape.

ENUMA ELISH, BOOK 4

Mithras Kills the Bull, Greek sculpture from c. 100/110 CE, symbolizing order defeating chaos in Persian myths.

Raging waters symbolized the formless chaos at the beginning of time.

THE BIBLE

Some of the same themes found in *Enuma Elish* can be found in the creation story in the first chapter of the book of Genesis. There is a watery chaos and darkness at the beginning; God speaks and there is light. The world is formed in stages, and humans are created last. The bare bones are similar, but there are profound spiritual insights that do not appear in the older myths. This story is monotheistic, with only one God. The chaos is abstract and impersonal (though the Hebrew word for chaos is *tehom*, from the same root as the Babylonian *Tiamat*). Humans are made to carry the power of God in the world, to be deputies looking after creation. This is the idea of being made 'in the image of God'.

They saw lakes and oceans, and springs bubbling up from under the earth.

Marduk slew Tiamat and carved up her body. Humans were created last of all, almost as an afterthought, to be slaves of the gods.

Solar myths

Solar myths depicted the power of light over darkness as that of life over death. The dying and rising theme is sometimes woven into these. The Egyptian Ra, the sun god, was said to sail through the underworld at night, and then he rose again in victory each morning, having fought off the demons and spirits of the dead.

Mithras was a god of light, the sun triumphant. He struggled with the chaos beast in the form of a bull. He slew the bull and its blood gave life to the earth. He was worshipped in temples with blazing torches and oil lamps fixed in his statues as though his light was shining out in blessing. This cult of Persian origin became very popular among the Romans, especially the legionaries.

Making Sense of Myths

Myths can be shown to contain powerful symbols and ethical directions. Their stories illuminate and guide the human spirit.

The American writer Joseph Campbell has written a four-volume study of myths called *The Masks of God* (1959–68). This suggestive title reminds us of the numinous power and transcendent hints found in mythical stories and rituals. They are masks that both hide and reveal the spiritual. Campbell found four key components in myths.

The first function is to relate our normal, waking consciousness with the vastness and mystery of the cosmos. Campbell uses a term coined by German scholar Rudolf Otto in his book *The Idea of the Holy* (1923), '*mysterium tremendum et fascinans*' ('the tremendous and fascinating mystery'). This is the sense of awe, of hairs standing up on the back of your neck, of trembling in the face of something stunningly beautiful. It is about looking up at the night sky and seeing how big it all is. It is stepping back in amazement at the first sight of a new baby.

The second function is interpretative. It seeks, as Shakespeare said, 'to hold, as t'were, a mirror up to nature'. It seeks to understand, to harmonize and to systematize.

The third function is ethical, sustaining a social order and one's place within a group. Moral codes expand into bodily adornment as well as taboos. Circumcision and tattoos can all be part of the lifestyle.

The fourth function is about personal growth and individuation: 'the centring and unfolding of the individual in integrity' according to the self, the community, the cosmos and the divine. Myths

It is not we who invent myth, rather it speaks to us as a Word of God.

CARL GUSTAV JUNG, *MEMORIES, DREAMS AND REFLECTIONS*

Jung dreamed of a 'spirit guide' that he called Philemon. He appeared as an old man with bulls' horns, kingfishers' wings and a bunch of four keys in his hand. These were ancient symbols of wisdom (old age), divinity (keys to open secret knowledge) and spiritual power (a bull's horn was a symbol of power in Ancient Near Eastern myths). The wings suggested god-like status, above the earth.

seek to locate us in the cosmos and within ourselves. Who are we and what can we become?

Archetypes

The Swiss psychologist Carl Jung (1875–1961) worked with a theory of archetypal images. These were potent symbols that kept on cropping up in myths and stories across cultures, and, intriguingly, in the dreams of his patients. They would imagine Greek gods or mythical figures.

Jung thought in symbolic terms. He wove his own forms of modern myth. One of the important archetypal images for Jung was 'the shadow'. The shadow is the repressed part of ourselves that we do not want to face up to. Thus, myths can live on in modern dress as powerful, potent stories and symbols. Myths are stories that are performed with symbols.

We must not deny our own shadow and project all our failings onto others 'out there'. If we do that, we demonize people and blind ourselves to our own evil.

Telling Stories

Human beings tell stories. It is in our nature. We tell stories about many things, such as the nature of the cosmos and society. Stories that embrace lofty themes are known as 'grand narratives'. Even in an age of science, we never stop being storytellers.

Science has need of the storyteller. Science might deal with objective facts as the result of observation and experiments, but how this data is processed and assembled involves a degree of imagination. Sometimes connections are made by flashes of insight, by subjective intuition, like Archimedes (c. 287–212 BCE) in his ancient Greek bath shouting, 'Eureka!'

Charles Darwin (1809–82) collected evidence for some degree of evolution on his travels on HMS *Beagle*. He had to fit it all together, to propose a theory, and theories are stories under another name. His story of the 'survival of the fittest' is a modern myth, a contemporary way of trying to make sense of the world. As scientists have gone on thinking and researching, aspects of Darwin's story have been changed and challenged, though it seems to remain the best story on offer to fit the facts, the best 'working hypothesis'. Perhaps

in another thousand years, a very different story will be told. Who knows?

James Bond?

Darwin's story has been abused by people who seek to eradicate the weak and deny them human rights. The Nazis were the worst example of this. We need to have a sense of value that cherishes life. Darwin would have argued that even his idea of survival meant that we

James Bond – the ultimate Darwinian?

Archimedes sat in his bath and shouted, 'Eureka!' when he suddenly realized how the physics of water displacement worked. Woodcut from 1547.

should help each other, for sharing a task and developing skills of cooperation help the human race to survive.

If there is no value system that endows the individual with rights of existence and treatment, then we live in a bleak world. The hi-octane adventures of fictional characters such as James Bond might be enjoyable, but they mask the reality that this is a hero who kills ruthlessly and sleeps around – the ultimate Darwinian, the fittest man. We need more than this to be human and for society to exist.

How do we live together?

Social theorists and economists tell stories about what sort of society we should live in. Karl Marx (1818–83) studied the vast sweep of human history and thought he discerned a pattern. Authoritarian societies would give way to capitalist ones with a free-market economy. This in turn must give way to a socialist system. He predicted that there would be an international workers'

> *We must, however, acknowledge, as it seems to me, that man with all his noble qualities, still bears in his bodily frame the indelible stamp of his lowly origin.*
>
> CHARLES DARWIN,
> *THE DESCENT OF MAN*, 1871

uprising that would create a communist state. This had great impact upon 20th-century politics, but his views are now regarded as simplistic by many. Maybe change is not inevitable. Some argue that capitalist democracy is the most enlightened form of social organization, with its liberty of conscience. In this sense, the 'end of history' is proclaimed. Perhaps this is just another story, another myth.

Summing up

Myths are more than primitive attempts to understand the world and natural phenomena. They contain deep insights and universal symbols that speak of awe, mystery and the inner dynamics of the psyche – the hopes and fears of humanity. As such, we will always need them to live by, and we will always be inveterate tellers of stories, even if they are based far more upon experimentation and reason.

21

THE GREEKS

Perhaps humans can never completely abandon mythological patterns of thinking, but the ancients, who explained things only in picturesque and animistic ways, actually explained little. The beginning of a more rational, scientific method of thought began, as far as anyone knows, in ancient Greece. Greece was the nexus of trade routes to the East and to the Mediterranean. Ideas and stories would have been trafficked about in a fairly cosmopolitan society.

The 6th century BCE saw the rise of philosophy in a stirring age of intellectual renaissance. Before this, the Greeks expressed their ideas in mythology. The epics of Homer and Hesiod (8th century BCE) told of the

Battle scene from a manuscript of the *Iliad* by Homer from c. 300 CE.

origin of the gods and the cosmos. In Hesiod's *Theogony*, many of the gods were representations of physical forces, but it was picturesque. It did not explain; it posited. Hesiod stated that there were four ages: gold, silver, bronze and iron. The gold was the perfect age when men were holy. Then there was a gradual decline until the present age. His ultimate beginning was something of a disappointment, for first of all there was 'the chasm' and then the earth. It was said that Epicurus (341–270 BCE) turned to philosophy in frustration at the

opening words from Hesiod. He asked the 'why' question that troubled his teachers.

Contents

First of all came the Chasm;
and then wide-bosomed Earth,
the eternal safe seat of all
the immortals who hold the heights
of snowy Olympus,
and murky Tartarus in the recesses
of the wide-pathed land,
and Love, who is fairest among
the immortal gods...

HESIOD, *THEOGONY*

The Pre-Socratics

The early Greek philosophers are often classed as 'the pre-Socratics' as they came before Socrates (470–399 BCE), who had an enormous influence on the development of philosophy.

The early philosophers have left very little in writing, mere scraps and fragments, or occasional mentions by later writers. We know a few names and a few of their key ideas.

Some of the early philosophers were eccentric: some were showmen, performing readings and poetry in garish clothes; some lived like hermits and some had disciples in mystical sects. It is possible that the love of spectacle derived from earlier rituals and shamanism. Indeed, some of the philosophers worked alongside the popular religions of the day, especially the mystery cults, from which some drew inspiration and insights. Others tended towards a more critical agnosticism, or even atheism.

Theologi and *physici*

Aristotle (384–322 BCE) wrote about the early philosophers as either *theologi* or *physici*: those who saw the gods as behind the powers of nature, and those who saw impersonal, physical

MYSTERY CULTS

The fertility cults of dying and rising gods developed into esoteric, secret cults called the mysteries. Initiates had to undergo purification and extensive rituals to seek union with the god and personal enlightenment. The initiates would descend into the depths of the temple, and undergo a ritual bath. They were brought back up again 'reborn', dressed in fine robes, with a crown of leaves and a burning torch in their hands. Some experienced visions and maybe trances in this state. As one philosopher stated, 'We beheld calm, happy, simple, eternal visions, resplendent in pure light.'

There was a sense, too, of a higher self and a lower self. Initiation sought to get in touch with the higher, more enlightened self.

forces. The *physici* questioned the myths as found in the works of Homer, for many of the actions of the gods were immoral. But we should not impose a modern, secular stance upon these early thinkers. To them, any great power that outlasted human lives, and was somehow foundational – the air or water, for example – was called 'divine', but it was not a about the nature of reality and sought to reduce it down to one simple force. Some believed this was air, some water, some fire, and one even argued that it was an invisible, undefinable substance. They were thinking in a new way, looking at the

Mystery cults initiated people into secret rites and experiences. *A Dedication to Bacchus* by Sir Lawrence Alma-Tadema (1836–1912).

personal deity. The crucial difference was that whereas some saw thunderbolts as being caused by the gods, others sought natural explanations – such as the build up of air in a cloud, which was discharged with a flash and a bang.

The early *physici* thought world with rational, analytical eyes. Perhaps their knowledge and ideas were limited, being so much guesswork, but they had begun a way of thinking that was to revolutionize the world.

> *If horses had hands and could draw, they would draw pictures of gods like horses.*
>
> XENOPHANES (c. 560–478 BCE)

What Are We?

The Milesian philosophers of the 6th century BCE sought an answer to the question, 'What is the world made of?'

Miletus was a prosperous city-state in the 6th century BCE, when the early philosophers were at work. It was a sea power with many colonies to the north. Its citizens were used to contact with new ideas and cultures, and some enjoyed periods of leisure. The question of what the earth is made from was hotly debated.

Water
Thales sought the answer in water. This can take different forms as liquid water, steam and ice. Living things are largely made up of water, and need it to flourish. Thales was in line with more ancient, mythological thinking too, in which everything came from water, from the abyss. Whether Thales also believed that everything was composed of water as a basic substance is a moot point. This would make water into an *arche*, a fundamental, 'divine' force. He observed that certain things, such as wood, float in water, and he speculated that the

earth floated in the same way. Thales is also famous for saying that magnets were alive, as they caused movement. It is easy to dismiss his views, but his was an early, enquiring mind that observed nature around him.

Is the world made of water, air or 'stuff'?

Animals come into being from moisture evaporated by the sun. Humans originally resembled another type of animal, namely fish.

HIPPOLYTUS, WRITING ABOUT ANAXIMANDER, *REFUTATION OF ALL HERESIES*

Air

Anaximenes looked to the air as the *arche*, the fundamental 'stuff' and origin of the cosmos. Breath is linked with life, and the ancients had similar words for breath and soul, or spirit. Homer spoke of the psyche ('soul') as 'the breath of life'. Fire was the most pure, 'thin' form, and rocks and mountains were the most condensed. Air and clouds were nearly pure. He saw the earth as a flat disk floating upon the air, and the stars were disks that had become so light that they were on fire, like the sun. Thunderbolts were explained as wind escaping from condensed clouds.

'Stuff'

Anaximander spoke of the *apeiron*, meaning 'the indeterminate'. He thought that the *arche* of the world was invisible, and that nature worked by a system of opposites such as light and dark, fire and water; there was a cosmic game of elements in conflict, recycling forces and substances as water absorbs fire, or as fire evaporates water and so on.

He thought that the flat earth was encircled by rings or wheels of fire. These rings are themselves surrounded by mist that has occasional holes in it, which allow the fire to shine out. We see these pinpricks of light as the sun and stars. Anaximander thought that the earth rested upon nothing; it was at the centre of a spherical universe and rested by means of equilibrium.

27

Mystical Numbers

Pythagoras was an enigmatic figure, a mathematician and logician mixed in with an esoteric philosopher and mystical teacher. For him, numbers revealed the foundations of reality.

Pythagoras was born around 580 BCE and lived for about 80 years. He lived, at first, on Samos, just to the north of Miletus. When he was in his forties, he emigrated to the Greek colonies in southern Italy, settling for much of his life in the city of Croton. He was exiled some years later, and many of his followers were persecuted. He founded a mystical, ascetic brotherhood, which cultivated intellectual study and followed various food taboos. He migrated from place to place, and his societies gradually died out after his demise. We have nothing in writing from him, but many

Basic mathematical concepts such as the equilateral triangle, with its equal angles and dimensions, came from Pythagoras. *Measuring of Angles with the Jacob's Staff*, woodcut, c. 1530.

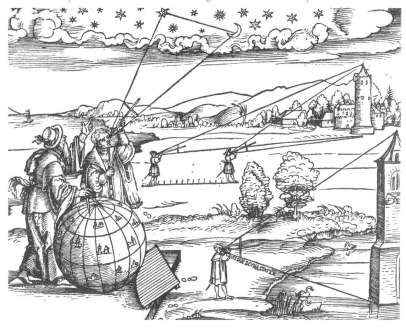

> *Pythagoras started a religion of which the main tenets were the transmigration of souls and the sinfulness of eating beans.*
>
> BERTRAND RUSSELL,
> *HISTORY OF WESTERN PHILOSOPHY*

Pythagoras is reported to have hated the idea of *pi*, for it showed an irregularity in the fundamental structure of the cosmos. It was an approximate, immeasurable number.

reports of his teachings exist from later times – though how far these are the views of later followers is debatable. Pythagoras is held to have said that the love of wisdom and a life of intellectual contemplation was an important way to spiritual liberation. He was the first to use the term 'philosophy', and was renowned for three basic teachings – reincarnation, the mystical nature of numbers, and food taboos.

He was more than likely a vegetarian (although he forbade the eating of beans!) as he believed that animals contained the souls of reincarnated friends and ancestors. His mysticism followed the cult of Orpheus, an intellectualized and ascetic form of Dionysus worship.

Numbers were important. He saw these as the fundamental *arche* of the universe. Everything could be reduced to mathematical order and harmony. The link between mathematics and music was also made – three musical chords favoured by the Greeks were explicable by three numerical ratios relating to the strings and the air vibrations caused. Pythagoras taught that while numbers were the *arche*, they, in turn, sprang from some other immaterial 'stuff' (remember Anaximander) to which numbers gave limit and order. Things were made of the 'one and the many' (fundamental substance and dimensions) or the 'unlimited and the limited'.

THE CULT OF ORPHEUS

Dionysus was a son of Zeus, born from union with Persephone. He was killed and eaten by the race of the Titans. Zeus punished the Titans by sending a thunderbolt against them. From their ashes, the human race sprang, a mixture of the divine and the evil of the Titans. Salvation lay in the hope of purification, and the body was seen as a prison for the soul. Matter was inferior and linked to the evil of the Titans. It was believed that the soul had to be purified to be set free at death, otherwise it would undergo purgatorial punishment. Orpheus was a mythical singer who taught the doctrines of salvation by this method – some of the hymns ascribed to him may have been written by Pythagoras.

The Riddler and the Rudder

Heraclitus was a member of the royal family based at Ephesus, north of Miletus. He was nicknamed 'the Riddler' and 'the Rudder', and these two epithets reveal the basic contours of his thought.

As 'the Riddler', Heraclitus (c. 540–480 BCE) was the writer of obscure sayings such as, 'Lifetime is a child at play, moving pieces in a game. Kingship belongs to the child.' Even Socrates could not understand all that he said, complaining that 'it needs a Delian diver to get to the bottom of it'. Heraclitus cast himself in the role of an enigmatic oracle, like that at Delphi, which gave no clear answers, but only suggestive signs. He was deliberately enigmatic and teasing in order to make people think.

As 'the Rudder', he taught that life and the world were in a constant state of flux. Nothing was permanent. All depended upon motion. Though all was in motion, all was one. He did not speculate upon the origin

The way up and down are one and the same.

HERACLITUS

of things, or the idea of a permanent, unchanging foundation, or *arche*. It was one reality that we perceived in flux, a dynamic movement of being. Fire burns, rises and moves, but it is still uniquely 'fire'. Life moves. Our concepts could only grasp aspects of reality and not totally pin them down.

NO TRUTH IS POSSIBLE?

Heraclitus was often misunderstood, and the more extreme views of one of his pupils, Cratylus, were propagated by later, influential writers as those of Heraclitus. Cratylus taught that everything was in such a radical state of flux that nothing could be examined – it did not stay the same for long enough – and no 'truth' was possible. Socrates rather mockingly called these views the dizziness of philosophers – they kept going round and round! Cratylus is said to have reached a position wherein he would not speak, but only moved his finger, for what sense could his words have? Heraclitus was more subtle: we can examine and predict much, but not everything; absolute, complete truth eludes us.

Fire moves, but it is one thing.

Conflict – the tension and play of opposites – was a fundamental principle of motion and growth for Heraclitus: we needed opposites: 'For there would be no attunement without high and low notes nor any animals without male and female.' They propelled things in a dynamic universe.

He rejected the idea of fire as the *arche*, because this would have been ever-changing, not static. This was an ethereal fire, different from the lower, earthly form we see burning. The human psyche was a part of this, animating the body, just as the *logos* ('reason')

> *You can't step into the same river twice.*
> HERACLITUS

animated the cosmos. Death came as the soul became too moist, but water was also life-giving, and new birth followed. Thus, all is one, the cosmos is a unity. Day and night are one too. Earlier myths cast darkness as an evil force, an absence of good and light, but for Heraclitus, day and night were part of a process, with days dawning and passing constantly.

Socrates

Socrates was a teasing, annoying, controversial thinker who attracted the young men of 5th-century Athens like a magnet. His searching questions in dialogue became influential as a method in future philosophy, and he has left behind an immense legacy, largely because of disciples such as Plato.

Socrates (470–399 BCE) was a poor man: his father was a stonemason, his mother a midwife and his wife a vegetable seller. He was detached and given to abstraction, sometimes standing for a whole day and night lost in thought. His critics argued that he was peddling his ideas

Roman sculpture of Socrates.

for money; he did not, although he courted wealthy friends and they often gave him lodging and nourishment. That one low-born could penetrate the higher echelons of Athenian society was amazing, and a testament to his charisma and

The ruined Temple of Apollo at Delphi, the site of the ancient oracle.

RELATIVISM AND SOPHISTRY

Socrates lived at a time of cultural expansion for the Greeks. The much-travelled Herodotus (484–424 BCE) presented the myths and beliefs of many races, and the Greek intelligentsia began to question their own traditions. Why should a thing be believed if others could see things differently? This cultural relativism spawned sophism as taught by Protagoras (490–420 BCE), a contemporary of Socrates. He said, 'Man is the measure of all things,' and disputed that any true, objective

knowledge was ever possible. All was relative, culturally conditioned and the partial construction of human thought and language. He added that wisdom was a set of skills to help people to see the world aright, and to present and win arguments. These skills could be taught, and the sophists earned their living in this way.

wisdom. The young men compared him to the river god Marsayas, whose flute enchanted all who heard it.

Many confused Socrates' ideas with sophism, such as his contemporary, the satirical playwright Aristophanes, who wrote a hilarious parody of Socrates in *The Clouds*. But Socrates was concerned to point people back to themselves, coaxing out honesty, humility and other virtues. He adopted the motto of the oracle at Delphi: 'Know thyself.' He attacked pomposity and cant, and always argued that he really knew nothing – though this was said in irony.

> *The unexamined life is not worth living.*
> SOCRATES

Socrates was snub-nosed with thick lips and bulging eyes. He poked fun at his own features, and once stood in a playful beauty contest. He argued that, as true beauty belonged to the inner man, and also to that which was more perfectly made (his nose could smell better, his eyes could see better), then he should win. He lost.

The Socratic Dialogues

Socrates' method of philosophical enquiry took the form of incisive, searching dialogues with friends and opponents. He was accused of atheism, impiety and corrupting the youth of his time.

There are four sources that tell us of Socrates' life and thought: the satirical play by Aristophanes, the later musings of Aristotle, and the works of Xenophanes and Plato, his contemporary followers. Xenophanes was the more pedestrian writer, recording basic stories and ideas, while Plato wrote copiously and often put his own ideas into the mouth of his master. A comparison of all these works reveals the true portrait of Socrates. He was an inveterate questioner, who would always set someone up. His victims/ subjects were invited to provide a definition of love or justice or beauty, and then Socrates would cross-examine them, exposing the shortcomings in their arguments. He sought rational truth; nothing could be trusted for its own sake. Sometimes he was playfully provocative; he did not always

The Death of Socrates by J.L. David (1748–1825).

reject the virtues he questioned, but was trying to get people to see how hard it was to define these concepts.

Trial and death

Socrates earned the nickname of 'the Gadfly' for his constant questioning and provocation. He courted powerful friends who fell foul of a change in the political situation. Athens had lost a long war with Sparta in 404 BCE, and the Spartans had installed a group of dictators known as the Thirty Tyrants. They were ruthless, executing many of their enemies. Socrates was a good friend of their leader, Critias, and another 'tyrant', Charmides. When a new democratic government was formed, accusations were made against Socrates: he had corrupted the youth of the city and had introduced new gods, being impious to the old ones. Socrates' questioning had made him some enemies. In reality, he seems to have sacrificed and prayed to the gods during civic rites and on special occasions. The 'new gods' probably referred to his personal, guiding spirit, his *daimonion*, most likely a personified form of conscience. Everything had to be questioned; nothing must be done that you did not believe was right. He claimed

> *Such… was the end of our comrade, who was, we may fairly say, of all those whom we knew in our time, the bravest and also the wisest and most upright man.*
>
> PLATO, *PHAEDO*

divine sanction for his work from Delphi, for an oracle had declared that there was none wiser in the land than Socrates. (He is said to have travelled around seeking to disprove this oracle by seeing if anyone could get the better of him in debate.) He sometimes spoke of 'God' as the one who really had all wisdom.

Eventually, the people of Athens held Socrates guilty, and he was sentenced to death by swallowing hemlock. He was surrounded by his friends as he did so, and his death was a courageous one. He had done what he believed was right and had no regrets. According to some accounts, he expressed hope for a life beyond death; in Plato's account, he produced a cluster of arguments in favour of immortality.

Plato

Plato, a disciple of Socrates, developed a philosophical system of his own that had far-reaching influence in the Greek world and afterwards.

Plato (427–347 BCE) was an Athenian aristocrat. He was present at the trial of Socrates and deplored what had happened. He left Athens in the early years of the restored democracy to work in Sicily as a tutor, and later returned to found an academy. His high-born social status led him to develop the idea of the philosopher-king, or an elite group who should run society.

Innate knowledge

Plato argued that human beings all have an innate knowledge of reality, not only as the rational faculty can perceive and work things out, but also from their many past lives (as the Pythagoreans taught). Learning is thus a form of remembrance of what we once knew, a type of memory or *anamnesis*.

Ideal forms

Plato believed that ideal forms lay behind everyday objects. A chair could exist in many forms on earth, but there was one basic template, one ideal quality of 'chairness', which was eternal. All beautiful things partake of the form of beauty. This unseen world of forms could be perceived by the wise philosopher through contemplation and the study of mathematics. Mathematics revealed eternal, constant properties in the flux and flow of the world; over the Academy entrance it said, 'No one ignorant of geometry admitted here.' Numbers and equations are constant; earthly forms are ephemeral. The beauty of numbers lasts forever, but the beauty of the individual snowflake is fleeting.

Politics

Plato's most renowned work is *The Republic*, his blueprint for a utopian society. In it, the figure of Socrates argues that a peaceful and harmonious state can only become possible when there is wise and benevolent leadership from a company of Guardians (both male and female) who are celibate, own no property and are dedicated to philosophy. The workers

and merchants live under normal conditions.

Plato's ideal state has been criticized as a form of dictatorship or tyranny; he rejected democracy as mob rule and compared the people to the crew of a ship that needed a strong captain, or a huge beast that needed taming. He also banished the poets from his ideal city, fearing that their emotive appeal would undermine the rule of reason.

THE CAVE

Plato told the parable of the cave in *The Republic*. He imagines that people are kept chained up in a cave, their faces turned towards the wall where they see shadows cast from the daylight behind them. They know nothing else and think that the shadows are reality. One day, one man escapes and turns to face the sunlight, running outside to see reality as if for the first time.

Plato argues that the average person lives in shadow, unenlightened. The wise man perceives that the ideal forms are behind the changing appearances of life. The radiance of the light is the light of reason, which we can find within our immortal souls.

Aristotle

Aristotle trained at Plato's Academy, but went on to develop his own, distinctly different ideas. He laid the foundations of modern science.

Aristotle (384–322 BCE) stayed at the Academy for 20 years, having arrived there at the age of 18. He left when Plato died, returning to his native Macedonia to tutor the king's 13-year-old son Alexander (later known as Alexander the Great). There, he married and settled, before eventually returning to Athens to found a rival school of philosophy, the Lyceum.

Aristotle developed a system of deductive logic based upon syllogisms with premises and conclusions, such as, 'All cats can purr. This is a cat. Therefore, this cat can purr.' He followed this with inductive logic, observing things in nature to see how

> *Humans are political animals.*
> ARISTOTLE

Athens, where Aristotle trained under Plato and founded his Lyceum.

they worked and deducing overarching principles.

Teleology

Aristotle rejected the Platonic theory of forms, arguing that there were only the actual objects in earthly existence. Instead, he collapsed the idea of participation in some greater type or force into their own being: they had an innate purpose or *telos* ('goal') within them. Thus, fire had the propensity to burn and to rise; heavy objects to fall. They exhibited final causes that acted as an internal drive or push to be what they were meant to be. Animals and human beings were much more complex in their *telos* or purpose. He saw a long chain of causes that led back to a First Cause or a Prime Mover.

THE DEMOCRAT

Aristotle criticized Plato's idea of a republic as a form of dictatorship. He rejected any utopian order on the grounds that as human beings are fallible their societies, in all their many forms, will also be imperfect. Thus, any autocrat will be dictatorial and self-serving to some extent. Aristotle wanted to share power among the people, as its diffusion would safeguard freedom.

Aristotle taught an ethical system of virtue against this political background. The 'good life' was to be learned by experience, by seeking to become a good citizen. People needed to choose the right path and not just to know what it was – here he parted from Socrates – and a series of right choices would produce good habits and character: the virtues. Right choices would be an avoidance of extremes and a mean. This idea of practising virtue was set against the backdrop of the Greek *polis*, the city-states of relatively small populations, where all were known to each other and could have a say in government.

Substance and soul

Following on from his teleological theory, Aristotle posited that each thing was essentially made of an invisible substance (the central question of earlier Greek thinking). A thing's substance can be separated into essential or accidental properties; fire had to burn, heat and rise to be fire, but its shape and colour were secondary accidents.

Aristotle argued that the soul is the animating or vital spark in each living thing, whether human, animal or vegetable. Vegetation had movement and growth; animals had sensations and humans also possessed reason. He seemed to be agnostic about the immortality of the human soul.

The Hellenistic Age

After Alexander the Great, Greek culture spread throughout the Mediterranean. The old politics and philosophy based in the city-states needed to be adapted to a new world order.

Alexander the Great (356–323 BCE) carved an empire across the Greek islands, through Egypt and Persia to the borders of India. His generals divided the territory between them and ruled. Eventually, these regions were taken over by the emerging Roman empire. Older ideas were disseminated, discussed and developed further.

Platonists and neoplatonists

Platonism went through various stages of development. The early form ran until the 3rd century BCE, continuing ideas faithfully after Plato. Middle Platonism made some adjustments and reconciled Plato with Aristotle on matters of ethics and logic. A developing metaphysics postulated two essential forces, the One and the Dyad (God and Matter). The forms had become ideas of God. (Greek philosophy had moved a polytheistic religion towards monotheism, whereby Zeus was often simply 'God'.) Other, intermediary orders were introduced, such as the World Soul and the demiurge. The latter was the creator of matter, sometimes seen as God, and sometimes as a lesser divine being, often called the *logos* ('reason'). Orders of daemons (intelligent spirits) were also at play in the structure of the world.

Neoplatonism developed later, under Plotinus (205–70 CE). He refined the concepts of Middle Platonism,

Alexander the Great, sculpture from the 2nd century BCE.

The whole divine economy is pervaded by Providence. Even the vagaries of chance have their place in Nature's scheme; that is, in the intricate tapestry of the ordinances of Providence. Providence is the source from which all things flow…

MARCUS AURELIUS,
MEDITATIONS, II:3

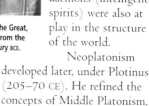

and taught a system whereby the One or the intellect gave being to the forms, and the soul was the lowest level of intelligence. Philosophy was to help the soul rekindle its spiritual and rational roots, and to prepare it for release from matter at death.

Stoics

Stoicism was founded by Zeno of Citium (c. 300 BCE), and it developed into one of the most influential Hellenistic philosophical systems alongside Platonism. Stoicism's three tenets were materialism, monism and mutation – everything had a share in physical being; there was an underlying, unifying substance; and everything changed constantly. The early Stoics have left little in writing, and we are reliant upon subsequent quotations. Later authors replicate their views, though, and prominent Romans such as Seneca (c. 4 BCE–65 CE) and the emperor Marcus Aurelius (121–80 CE) followed Stoicism. Basically, Stoics held that God, Spirit or the *logos* permeated the cosmos and dwelt within each human soul. Matter was ordered in the best possible way, and events were preordained in the best possible way, though our individual actions were still (somehow) free. There would be cyclic periods of history with cosmic conflagrations and renewals. All was composed of mystical fire, light or spirit, and the changing forms of earthly life were fleeting appearances and shapes derived from the fire. When they collapsed back into that, they were destroyed, but new creation would come forth in due course.

Individuals needed to 'tune in' to the *logos* within, and to seek to live in harmony with it. The *logos* thus functioned as a mixture of conscience, intuition and reason.

Thus, the major themes of Greek philosophy were reflected in Stoicism – the 'Big Question' of what everything was made of; the quest for the 'good life'; and the hope of freeing the soul from falsehood, and to embrace whatever lay beyond death.

Summing up

Greek philosophy engaged reason and logical analysis as never before in the history of humanity, and it can be said to have laid the foundations for Western thought and the eventual rise of modern science. We see debates and different emphases, however, which turn to a more sceptical, materialistic explanation of the world, but there are those who allow for a more mysterious and mystical aspect. Such debates and feelings are still with us.

WISDOM FROM THE EAST

Just as Greece was a fertile area for early philosophy, so were the lands of the East: the Indian subcontinent, China, Japan and Asia Minor. There are debates about how far ideas trafficked between Greece and the East. There are some similarities and possible influences, but distinctive ideas emerged.

Indian civilization goes back to at least 3000 BCE. Archaeologists have excavated Mohenjo-Daro, a city in the Indus valley with paved streets and brick houses. There was a

Chinese silk tapestry from c. 1600, made for the front of an altar.

drainage system and running water. Clay seals and inscriptions reveal images of some of the gods of later Hinduism. The term Hindu refers to the area of the River Indus and was first used by the Persians. Hindus refer to their faith and philosophy as the *Sanatana Dharma*, the 'eternal law' or 'way'. Hinduism developed over the centuries as different tribal groups invaded and settled. New ways, rituals, gods and ideas entered a pool of spiritual thought.

Chinese culture goes back as far as that of India. It has a different emphasis; harmony and balance are paramount. The gods have their roles, but they are not as central as they are in Hindu mythology and thought. There was no state religion, though philosophies were revered and handed down with a similar devotion. The Chinese language remained unchanged for centuries, enabling this faithful transmission to take place. There is more emphasis on the 'good life' and how to act, rather than questions of absolute truth.

Contents

Love the Lord and be free. He is the One who appears as many, enveloping the cosmos, without beginning or end.

THE UPANISHADS

The Vedas

The Vedas are the earliest Hindu scriptures. 'Veda' means 'knowledge'. The ideas contained in these scriptures developed over the centuries.

Vedantic knowledge developed in stages from the prehistoric era, through a period of foreign invasion (c. 2000 BCE) and into the main era (1500–700 BCE). The Vedic system came with these invaders, and the Aryan people transmitted the Vedas orally at first. The earliest text was the Rig Veda, composed between 1500 and 900 BCE, a collection of hymns and details of sacrifices. Some key Hindu ideas began to emerge in this period:

KEY HINDU IDEAS

At the root of our troubles lies *avidya* ('ignorance'); *vidya* ('wisdom') will bring *bodhi* ('enlightenment') and *moksha* ('release'). This life is *maya* ('illusion'), and clinging to the flesh and the passions is the way of death. Countless rebirths will allow someone to scale the heights of karma and then they will achieve *moksha*, joining with the life force Brahman beyond all form and change.

Lead me from the unreal to the real;
Lead me from the darkness to light;
Lead me from death to immortality.
THE UPANISHADS

◆ The caste system – this established a strong, social hierarchy that determined occupations and marriage, for example. The different levels reflected different professions – priests, warriors, traders, unskilled workers. Those outside the caste system, the Dalits, or untouchables, have few rights. No one knows where they came from.
◆ Karma – this means the effect of your deeds in life, not 'fate'. We buy into it by how we act. A person's caste, for example, is determined by their karma in a previous life.
◆ Reincarnation – Hindu thought has always held the idea of the transmigration of souls, whereby a soul can be reborn as a human or an animal (and some would add as a vegetable too).

The Vedanta

This means 'the end of the Vedas' and includes texts written towards 700 BCE, including the Upanishads. These are philosophical texts that are sometimes in dialogue form. 'Upanishad' means 'sitting down near', from the disciple who sat at the feet of a teacher, or guru. Concepts of

God and the soul take on a new meaning in these texts. Brahman is the unseen life force behind all things, and *atman* is the soul within a person, but also a part of the divine, a spark of Brahman within us. The Upanishads tend to see the gods as aspects of Brahman; God becomes more impersonal and abstract, a force.

The epics

The heroic sagas – the *Mahabharata* and the *Ramayana* – were written during the Epic Age, which stretched from about 800 to 200 BCE. The *Mahabharata* is set in ancient India and is about a struggle for the throne. One section of this became popular in its own right – the *Bhagavadgita* (*Song of the Lord*) which is a dialogue between Krishna and Arjuna before one of many battles. Krishna is Prince Arjuna's charioteer, who reveals himself as divine by the end of the text. The epics contain the idea of avatars, divine appearances on earth in the form of animals or humans. These are of the god Vishnu, whom some worship simply as 'God'. The divine appearances all take place in a timeless, undatable era, and the avatars are not real incarnations, but disguises. The god cannot be hurt in any way.

That You Are!

Unlike Greek thought, the key question for Hindu philosophy was not 'What "stuff" is the cosmos made of?' but 'What is the true self?' and 'What is real at all?'

The Upanishads taught that the true self is a part of a much greater whole, the life force called Brahman. Each *atman*, or 'soul', is a spark of this divine force. One master taught his disciple about Brahman. He asked him to take some salt and pour it into a bowl of water. He was asked to taste the water from different corners of the bowl. Did he taste the salt? He did from every angle he tried. The master replied that this is the nature of Brahman: in all things. Then he added, *'Tat tvam asi'* ('That you are'). The Vedanta taught that we are really 'God' at our deepest level of being. It is rather like peeling an onion and reaching the innermost layer.

Yoga

Yoga means 'union', and there are various forms of yoga that seek union with God: karma yoga is a way of good works and virtue; jnana yoga is about bodily self-control and meditation; and bhakti yoga is about praise and devotion to God.

The Western practice of hatha yoga as a means of exercise and healthy living is the first stage of the disciplines

> *Peacefulness, self-control, austerity,*
> *purity, tolerance, honesty,*
> *knowledge, wisdom and*
> *religiousness — they are the*
> *qualities by which the Brahmins*
> *work righteousness.*
>
> BHAGAVADGITA

Yoga seeks union with God. Hindu illustration demonstrating the lotus position, from a series with depictions of the yoga technique in Hindu verse.

that lead to bodily control and meditation.

Bhakti

Bhakti yoga teaches a way of personal devotion to a personal deity. The impersonal divine force of the Upanishads might appeal to sages, but not to the ordinary person. Bhakti devotees dance, sing and chant praises. They worship God in one particular form, be it Vishnu or Shiva or Krishna. Their personal way is their *ishta devata* ('chosen way'). They do not necessarily reject the *ishta devata* of others who worship God by a different name. Bhakti flourished in the Middle Ages, and Krishna's cause was promoted by the sage Caitanya (1486–1534) in Bengal. He was converted by following a devotee of Krishna and formed a community at Puri. He taught that Krishna was the Supreme Godhead, and not just one form of Vishnu. The way

to worship was to chant the divine praises: 'Hare Krishna, Hare Krishna, Krishna, Krishna, Hare, Hare. Hare Rama, Hare Rama, Rama, Rama, Hare, Hare.' Here we have the divine names of Krishna and Rama, another appearance of Vishnu, as well as Hare, a name for Radha, the faithful consort of Krishna. The International Society for Krishna Consciousness, devotees of which are commonly known as Hare Krishnas, teaches this way to union with God.

The bhakti movement challenged some religious ideas. The caste system should be based upon inner ability and character, and not simply on birth. This is supported by a passage in the *Bhagavadgita*.

Buddhism

Buddhism began in India, with its roots in Hinduism and the Vedas, but rejected key elements and adopted a popular, easily accessible style of teaching and worship.

The Buddha (meaning 'Enlightened One') was Siddhartha Gautama (c. 536–476 BCE). He left a life of luxury in a palace as a young man to seek inner truth and peace. He joined a group of ascetic holy men in the forests for a while, fasting and almost starving himself. He left these men to find truth on his own, and he experienced 'enlightenment' or 'awakening'

No self?

The Buddha's *anatman* doctrine sounds rather like some postmodern ideas that the self is a fiction, such as the teaching of the psychologist Jacques Lacan (1901–81). Lacan stated, 'The self is a sign,' and he saw the 'self' as a social construction from language and inner images in social interaction. Still, the Buddha was evasive; he may have seen a substance behind the illusions. Other thinkers argue that there is a mystery to the self, which is only partly a social construction. Here, we are moving beyond words.

while sitting in meditation under a bo tree. This led to an itinerant ministry for 49 years.

The *anatman*
The Buddha questioned the idea of the *atman*. Instead of seeing a permanent essence at the core of each person, he saw impermanence and illusion. He taught the *anatman*, the 'no-self'. We are clusters of drives, hopes, fears and karmic forces from our actions in this life and previous ones. He taught

reincarnation – not of a permanent soul, but of this bundle of forces. The awakened person moved beyond these, seeing that the mind was pure and more than the ego. This inner state of release, of

> *Those whose minds have reached full excellence in the factors of enlightenment, who have renounced acquisitiveness, rejoice in not clinging to things – glowing with wisdom, they have attained nirvana in this very life.*
>
> THE BUDDHA

Young Buddhist monks with their master in the Tashiding Cloister, Sikkim, East Innida.

awakening, was known as nirvana. This word comes from the idea of being cool. Stepping out from the midday sun into the cool shade is one analogy used by the Buddha.

Teachings of the Buddha

The Buddha's teaching is summed up by the three jewels: the Buddha, dharma and the sangha. The Buddha shows that a person can reach enlightenment and inner peace; dharma is the truth, the law of life (expressed by the four noble truths, below); the sangha is the community of monks, open to men and women equally, and to anyone of any caste. The Buddha rejected the caste system.

The four noble truths are as follows. *Dukkha* ('suffering') is everywhere; it is a part of existence. *Dukkha* is caused by wrong desires, lusts and selfish grasping. There is a way out; liberation from suffering is possible. The path to freedom is the eightfold path: right understanding; right thought; right speech; right action; right living; right endeavour; right mindfulness; and right concentration.

This ethically and spiritually healthy lifestyle was a 'middle way', rejecting extreme asceticism and luxury. It sought balance, poise and harmony. In this, the Buddha was akin to Aristotle, who taught the Golden Mean in ethics.

Types of Buddhism

Different versions and schools of Buddhism spread after the Buddha's death. Some added to his ideas, or argued that they had interpreted him more thoroughly.

The Buddha was silent about many issues, and enigmatic at other times. He refused to be drawn on the metaphysical speculations and disputes in Hinduism. He taught that dharma must be put before the gods; lifestyle came before beliefs. He seemed to say that there was an eternal, unborn state that was akin to pure mind; was nirvana a blissful eternity? Different schools of Buddhism sprang up after the Buddha's death. Some were minimalist, such as the Theravada school, avoiding metaphysics and seeming to be almost materialistic and atheistic. Others, such as the Mahayana school, which spread to Asia, added beliefs, rituals and speculations. Tibetan Buddhism enriched the Buddha's teaching in yet more exotic ways, and Zen in Japan brought a new interpretation.

Theravada

Theravada means 'the teaching of the elders', and it is the earliest form of Buddhism. It is based upon the earliest

Better it is to live one day virtuous and meditative than to live a hundred years immoral and uncontrolled.

THE BUDDHA

Tibetan monks carry a portrait of the Dalai Lama, who is believed to be a reincarnation of the Buddha.

collection of teachings of the Buddha, at first oral and then written down in the Pali language.

Mahayana

Mahayana means 'great vehicle'. The term 'vehicle' refers to the idea that dharma is like a raft that carries us across the ocean of life. The Mahayana movement began with groups that broke away from the rest of Buddhism over certain

ZEN BUDDHISM

Zen Buddhism (or Ch'an, in China) traces its roots back to the 6th century CE, when missionaries came from India to China. It was a wisdom movement, relying on personal intuitions and teaching passed from master to disciple, rather than rituals and writings. Writings are inferior to truth in the heart. Zen developed the koan, the short, pithy saying that opens up awareness, such as 'Can you hear the sound of one hand clapping?' It took root in Japan from about 1200 CE.

interpretations and rules. These groups gathered momentum and evolved new ideas. Key thoughts of the Mahayana are only attested in writing from the beginning of

the Christian era, and it is not clear how far back their teachings go. It is intriguing that some aspects of Mahayana are akin to Christianity:

◆ The virtue of compassion is emphasized more than in early Buddhism.
◆ There is a series of heavenly or cosmic Buddhas who choose to take flesh and teach humanity – the bodhisattvas.
◆ Some groups had an eschatology, a doctrine of the last things. They hoped for a new Buddha who was to come: Maitreya, the 'loving one'.

Interestingly, it was the areas of India open to trade with the Mediterranean that developed Mahayana Buddhism. The Mahayana is largely confined to the northern hemisphere of the Buddhist world, and the Theravada to the south.

The Buddha was once asked why evil existed. He replied that if you found a man who had been shot by a poisoned arrow, then you would be more concerned to pull it out and heal him than to ask who did it. The Buddha showed a simple pragmatism, avoiding difficult questions, and he in fact died after eating poisonous mushrooms.

Confucius

Confucius, or K'ung fu-tzu, was a contemporary of the Buddha. Though only one of a number of famous teachers in his day, his philosophy defined Chinese culture from then on.

The Ancient Period of Chinese culture, up to 200 BCE was described as the time of the Hundred Schools. These originated at the royal court, with various groups competing for ideas. We know little about Confucius (551–479 BCE) with any certainty; the first biography of him dates from 300 years after his death. Scholars are divided as to the extent of his writings. Some claim he wrote all of the Six Classics, covering the liberal arts. Others argue that he might have edited these, but only the *Analects* are from him.

The Master said, 'He who rules by moral force is like the pole-star… Govern the people by regulations, keep order among them by chastisements, and they will flee from you, and lose all self-respect. Govern them by moral force, keep order among them by ritual and they will keep their self-respect and come to you of their own accord.'

ANALECTS, BOOK II

THE *ANALECTS*

The *Analects* were a series of aphorisms written down by the disciples of Confucius; they recorded the teaching of others as well, and incidents from their lives. How many of the sayings of 'the Master' were genuinely from Confucius is debatable. Chinese philosophers taught in the style of the short, suggestive saying or question. They did not follow the expository, discursive reasoning of the Greeks or the metaphysical speculations of India.

Do not do to others what you do not wish yourself.

CONFUCIUS, *ANALECTS*

Some disagree even with this. Confucius seems to have worked in government, and then taught sometimes thousands of students in retirement.

The *chun-tzu*

The *chun-tzu* was the son of a lord, a nobleman. Confucius redefined this to emphasize inner qualities. He thus cut across social boundaries and invited anyone who was willing to seek a life of virtue. Indeed, he said that a son of a nobleman who did not live up to his calling was not a true *chun-tzu*. Confucius's disciple Mencius (371–289 BCE) argued that an unrighteous ruler should be overthrown by the people: 'The

Confucius as a teacher, Chinese woodcut from about the 6th century BCE.

people are the most important element in a state...' Mencius's ideas were approved of in Maoist China, many years later.

Confucius was silent about the gods and metaphysical questions. He taught an ethical way that sought compassion and justice. An individual should seek harmony; society needed to be based upon personal righteous acts. Chinese religion was traditionally based upon ancestor worship rather than the worship of gods. Rituals and gifts were necessary to assuage the ancestors. Confucius reinterpreted these to show respect for the different orders of society, the ancestors included.

Jen, *li* and *chih*

The quest for balance and harmony could be broken down into three principles: *jen* – being righteous within; *li* – laws and social etiquette; and *chih* – right behaviour.

Jen is the goal, for all else comes from this (rather like the Christian Augustine's maxim, 'Love God and do as you will'). *Jen* must be followed by right behaviour in the five orders of human relationships as understood in Chinese culture: parent and child; ruler and advisor; elder and younger siblings; husband and wife; and friend and friend.

The *Tao*

The *Tao*, or Way, is a key element in Chinese philosophy, pre-dating the works of Confucius and Lao Tzu.

The *Tao Te Ching* is the most famous and influential philosophical work next to the teaching of Confucius. *Tao* means 'way' or 'path'; *Te* means 'power of virtue' or 'moral force'; and *Ching* means 'classic'. Hence, *Tao Te Ching* means 'The Classic Text of the Way of Virtue'. This is said to have been written in the 6th century BCE by a man about whom we know next to nothing – Li Erh Tan, who was given the honorific title of Lao Tzu (meaning 'Old Master'). Legend has it that he wrote the text in one night and then travelled west, never being heard of again. It is a collection of aphorisms, wise sayings that try to suggest what is meant by *Tao*, and how to follow it and harness the power of *Te*. Some of its concerns sound very like those of Confucius, seeking to be in harmony with the *Tao* to build harmony in society.

Tao had a mystical leaning in the works of Lao Tzu and later Taoist philosophers. The *Tao* was an immaterial, undefinable force that was before all things and flows through all things. It cannot be described, only lived.

Sung dynasty statue of Lao Tzu riding a water buffalo.

Wu-wei

One principle of the *Tao* is to 'go with the flow'. *Wu-wei* can

Tao is not a way that can be pointed out.
Nor an idea that can be defined.
Tao is indefinable original totality.
Ideas create the appearance of separate things.
Always hidden, it is the mysterious essence.
Always manifest, it is the outer appearances.
Essence and appearance are the same.
Only ideas make them separate.
Mystified?
Tao is mystery.
This is the gateway to understanding.

LAO TZU, *TAO TE CHING*

be translated as 'non-action', but this is misleading. It sounds like fatalism and passivity. It is a way of 'letting be', or facing reality, of staying calm and working with what you have. It is about accepting what you cannot change, and seeking to change that which you can alter, gently and carefully. An early Taoist, Yang Chu, stated that he would not exchange being ruler of the world for one hair from his back. In other words, he accepted who he was and where he was, and sought to treasure the simple things of life that were given and free — a smile, the beauty of nature, friendship and so on. This talk of 'letting be' and of simplicity was often misunderstood as selfish inaction and pietism.

Reversal

One principle of the *Tao* is that humans must seek to live in harmony with the underlying laws of nature. One such law, according to Lao Tzu, is that of reversal. When something is pushed to extremes, it turns into its opposite, such as night and day, hot and cold.

The *Tao* is an undefinable force that flows through all things.

Taoism has been the preserve of scholars and monks rather than the common people, unlike Confucianism. The most popular use of the *Tao Te Ching* is as a talisman to ward off sickness or spirits.

Cooking a small fish and ruling a
big country need equal care.
When the world is ruled by Tao,
Evil is powerless.
Not that it doesn't exist.
It just has no power to harm people.
The Wise don't want anyone to
come to harm.
When people don't hurt each other,
Natural Goodness spreads through
the land.

LAO TZU, *TAO TE CHING*

55

Learning from the East

Eastern philosophy has become more widely known in the West, and the challenges of new technology and ideas can be enhanced by some Eastern insights.

Westerners dressed as Krishna devotees and emblems such as the yin-yang on necklaces and fashion items are a superficial sign of a blending of East and West. Aspects of Eastern thought have been taken up by the New Age movement, seeking a spiritual path amid Western materialism and cynicism.

There are several ways in which Eastern philosophy has prefigured insights of modern science or postmodern thought.

Interconnectedness

Eastern philosophy stresses that all things are interconnected. Reality is a whole. The Zen teacher Dogen (1200–1253 CE) said that objects have no intrinsic meaning. They are 'nothing' if not understood as related to other things. Truth is in the relation, the 'and' and the 'other'. Western thought has sought to classify and isolate material objects, breaking them down and down into the smallest units possible.

Holistic science, medicine and philosophy teach interconnectedness; the whole is greater than the sum of the parts. Life is a totality that cannot be broken down and defined. The growing flower is killed and diminished by plucking it and stripping it apart under a microscope.

> *Buddha-nature is vast emptiness, open, clear and bright.*
>
> DOGEN, THE ZEN MASTER

Change

Eastern thought stresses the impermanence of all things; all

Western women practising yoga.

56

is *maya* ('illusion'). Life is fluid, to be lived forwards; the *Tao* flows through all things. There is also a sense of underlying permanence, of foundation, of Brahman, *Tao* or karma. The non-discursive manner of Eastern philosophy can cope with paradox, mystery and playfulness. Western science, since the advent of quantum mechanics and the new physics, imagines a world less solid and 'real' than previous generations had sensed. All is a dance of subatomic particles whose patterns and trajectories cannot always be predicted. Chairs and tables are moving around, never still, if only we had eyes powerful enough to see. The human body is largely made up of water, after all!

A wheel is useful, because of the hole at the centre of the hub.
A clay pot is useful, because it contains empty space.
Doors and windows are useful, because they are gaps in the walls.
The value of what is there lies in what is not there!

LAO TZU, *TAO TE CHING*

female. This, in turn, was challenged by certain postmodern thinkers, arguing that there are some things that defy such categorization. New philosophy has challenged key ideas of East and West together.

Opposites attract?

The ancient Chinese principle of yin-yang, assumed by Lao Tzu and Confucius, was based upon the sun and the night – yang being the sunlight and yin the opposite. Yin is feminine and yang masculine. All things have their opposite, and in this dialectic there is a creative harmony. Twentieth-century structuralists, such as Claude Lévi-Strauss, coined the term bipolarity, seeing the cosmos as a system of opposites at play, such as hot and cold, male and

Summing up

Eastern philosophy (and the religion it is usually intricately interwoven with) has some overlap with Greek thought, but it has developed a more mystical, picturesque and suggestive approach. 'That which cannot be said' is as important as 'that which can be said', rather as a hole in the centre of a wheel allows the mechanism to work. In this way, many of the preoccupations of postmodern thought were anticipated. We are only humbly human, 'bears of little brain', to paraphrase *Winnie the Pooh*.

THE CHRISTIAN ERA

The Romans carved out an empire that included North Africa, much of Europe, and the Near East as far as the borders of Persia. The emperor Augustus held sway over this huge empire until his death in 14 CE. With his rule, the empire entered a long period of stability called the Pax Romana – lands under Roman control enjoyed prosperity, and increased communications and trade.

The idea of the divine ruler was common in the East. Alexander the Great had been hailed thus in Egypt, and the emperors of Rome, beginning with Julius Caesar, used this to foster loyalty and unity. Refusal to offer sacrifice to the emperor could be construed as treason.

Madonna and child with Emperor Justinian (left), holding a model of Hagia Sophia, and Emperor Constantine (right), holding a model of Byzantium. Sixth-century mosaic from Hagia Sophia, Istanbul, Turkey.

Besides the cult of the emperor, there were the traditional gods of Rome. Great efforts were made to identify different national deities with the Roman pantheon to encourage unity. Myths of demigods or divine men took on a new energy as it became the vogue to call any outstanding leaders, philosophers or holy men 'divine', meaning that something of the light or power of God was at work in them.

The philosophical schools looked upon popular religious and mystery cults, such as Mithraism, somewhat sceptically. These cults often spoke of 'God' as a singular concept – as the light of reason or the power of fate. They were edging towards a form of monotheism.

This was the context in which Christianity was born. People were searching for release from oppressive rulers and the power of fate. The poor sought healing and food; intellectuals were moving towards belief in one God. Jesus of Nazareth spoke to all these needs and began a radically new spiritual movement.

Contents

For God so loved the world that he gave his one and only Son, that whoever believes in him shall not perish but have eternal life.

JESUS, JOHN 3:16

The Jews

One race within the Roman empire was spared the obligation of ruler worship, and great respect was given to their refusal to use sacred images in worship – the Jews.

The Jews were an ancient people, descended from a group of Semitic tribes in the land of Canaan – the original name of the area that became the 'Holy Land', or modern-day Palestine and Israel. Some of their ancestors had been slaves in Egypt for generations, but a charismatic leader, Moses, led them into the Sinai desert to freedom (possibly 15th or 13th century BCE – opinions vary). They told and retold the story in song, liturgy and in sacred meal. This 'exodus' was the foundational event of their faith. The story was told of how God had spoken to Moses, using the name 'Yahweh', which meant 'I am who I am'. The tribes had called God by the common Near-Eastern term 'El' before this. Moses had assembled the people at Mount Sinai, and there, in gratitude, they had bound themselves to serve Yahweh and to follow his Way or Law ('Torah' in Hebrew.) The core of the Torah was the Decalogue, the ten commandments, with their religious and social obligations.

They also believed that Yahweh had chosen them and bound himself to them, and this binding relationship was known as a covenant. Earlier traditions too, before the exodus, had spoken of promises and blessings by El on their ancestors, such as Abraham. The Jews developed an early idea of monotheism, that there was only one God, and that time was not cyclical, always repeating itself like the seasons. Time had a direction, a goal, and the world had a purpose.

Prophets, kings and exiles

The tribes established themselves in Canaan and grew into a great power, united under King David at the end of the 1st millennium BCE. Tribal and religious differences led to infighting and the division into a northern and a southern kingdom, Israel and Judah. Israel was defeated by Assyria in the 8th century BCE, and the people were scattered, never to return. Judah survived, but was eventually conquered by Babylon in the 6th century

Of the ten commandments, the first four are religious commandments, dealing with the unique nature of God and the day that was to be dedicated to him, and the remaining six are social in focus.

The biblical account of the parting of the Red Sea is less magical than often depicted in art or films. Exodus 14:21 states that the waters parted after a strong wind blew all night. It did not happen in an instant. *The Rescue of the Israelites and the Drowning of the Egyptians in the Red Sea.* Woodcut by Julius Schnorr von Carolsfeld (1794–1874) from *The Bible By Pictures.*

BCE. Many people were taken into exile, but they were to return years later under the benevolent reign of Cyrus, the king of Persia. Jerusalem was then rebuilt and the kingdom restored. After the restoration, the Jews did not have the freedom or resources that they once enjoyed. Kings ruled under the influence of foreign powers, such as the Greeks and then the Romans. By the time of Jesus, Rome ruled the land directly through officials.

Prophets spoke of future judgment, the 'Day of the Lord', and the dawning of an age of blessing. Connected with these was the hope of a future king, the Messiah. 'Messiah' simply meant 'anointed one', and every Jewish king was a messiah in the sense that they were anointed with holy oil at their coronation. The Messiah was to be anointed above all the others, with the power of God to liberate the people and to bring blessings to the earth.

The Jews in the 1st century CE

The Jews had been under Roman rule since 63 BCE, and many groups sought to oust the foreign overlords. Messianic hopes were alive, and messianic pretenders took up arms.

The focal point of Jewish worship was the temple in Jerusalem. The temple was based upon the simple tent layout that Moses had used in the desert. By the time of Jesus, it was a highly elaborate, beautiful and rich building. It was in three sections – the court of the Gentiles, the court of the women and the court of the Israelites. Only Jewish men were allowed within the third. Within this was the sanctuary where the priests ministered. This in turn housed the Holy of Holies, where Yahweh was thought to specially dwell. Prayers, incense, grain and animal

Scale model showing the temple compound in Jerusalem at the time of Herod the Great (c. 20 BCE).

He [Pilate] was cruel and his hard heart knew no compassion. His day in Judea was a reign of bribery and violence…

PHILO OF ALEXANDRIA,
LEGATIO AD GAIUM

offerings were made daily in the sanctuary, but only the high priest entered the Holy of Holies once a year on the day of atonement, to offer sacrifice for the forgiveness of the people.

Zealots and parties

There were four different religious schools of thought among the Jews at the time of Jesus. The landed gentry were the Sadducees, trying to keep the status quo; the Pharisees were a devout group of scholars and teachers; the Zealots were revolutionaries ready to take up arms against the Romans; and the Essenes were a separatist sect with their own rituals, who rejected the temple cult in Jerusalem. It is likely that a group of Essenes lived in the Qumran community that gave us the Dead Sea Scrolls.

Various armed uprisings were attempted, such as that of Judas the Galilean in 6 CE. He protested against paying taxes to Rome, as the land belonged to the Jews. The largest revolt

IIn the 1st century BCE, King Herod the Great restored the temple, adding extra colonnades and walls of marble, with richly embroidered tapestries inside. Herod was a convert to Judaism and was seen by many Jews as impious and lax with the Torah. Some Jews rejected his temple and the cult that went with it.

PILATE AND THE JEWS

Pontius Pilate was the Roman prefect or governor of Judea from 26–36 CE. He was a ruthless and unpopular man. When he arrived, his legions marched into Jerusalem carrying standards bearing the image of the emperor; the Jews objected to these as idolatrous. Pilate sat on his judgment seat the next day, and invited the protesting mob to state their case before him. He surrounded them with soldiers and threatened to cut them to pieces unless they relented. They simply fell to the ground as a body and bared their necks, thus showing that they were ready to die for their Law. Pilate then backed down.

took place in the middle of the 1st century, and Jerusalem was besieged and destroyed in 70 CE. Only one part of the temple was left standing, the present-day Western Wall.

Jesus of Nazareth

Jesus was a wandering, charismatic teacher and healer who drew the crowds. Many hoped he was the Messiah.

Jesus lived from about 4 BCE to 33 CE. The exact date of his birth cannot be ascertained. Although the Western dating scheme is based upon him, a 6th-century monk, Dionysius Exiguus, made a mistake and missed out some years of one of the emperors. Biblical texts tell us that Jesus was born before Herod died; this was in 4 BCE. His actual Aramaic name would have been Yeshua bar Yosif ('Jesus, son of Joseph').

There are four accounts of his life in the New Testament. The books about Jesus are called Gospels, from a Greek word meaning 'good news'. They have their differences and their own ideas, but they overlap in many ways. The first three, Matthew, Mark and Luke use much of the same material; John has some different traditions and seems more philosophical or spiritual. They all reveal a consistent portrait of Jesus as a holy man who broke many of the religious and social taboos of his day, eating with tax collectors (who were shunned because they worked for the Romans), speaking with harlots, and touching lepers. He spoke of the coming kingdom of God, which sometimes was a supernatural event breaking into human history, and at other times sounded like an inner realization, something that was within us if only we sought it. God was known as 'Father', or, in Aramaic, 'Abba'. Jesus knew an intense and intimate relationship with God.

> *The kingdom of God is within you.*
> JESUS, LUKE 17:21

The Messiah?

Jesus kept on avoiding the issue

THE LORD'S PRAYER

Jesus' own prayer summarized his main teachings. God was a Father; the kingdom was to come; and forgiveness was central to a holy life:

> Our Father in heaven,
>   hallowed be your name,
> your kingdom come,
> your will be done
>   on earth as it is in heaven.
> Give us today our daily bread.
> Forgive us our debts,
>   as we also have forgiven our debtors.
> And lead us not into temptation,
>   but deliver us from the evil one.

Before Jesus began preaching, he was described as a *tekton*, a Greek word that could mean 'joiner', 'carpenter', 'builder' or even 'architect'. Scholars dispute his social status. He may have been one of the artisan class, landless and dependent upon local hire, or of a lower-middle-class business family.

Manuscript illumination of Christ's crucifixion from the 15th century.

of whether he was the Messiah or not. If people called him by that title, he asked them to be quiet; when he was tempted in the wilderness, he seemed to have rejected common understandings of the role as a mighty man who would do great signs and wonders. The term 'Christ', the Greek form of Messiah, was never used by him and was not his proper name. It was a title given to him by his followers.

His preaching and popularity brought him to the attention of the Romans, and his statements against the temple – 'Destroy this temple, and I will raise it again in three days ' (John 2:19) – outraged the Jewish leaders, who feared that he would start a rebellion when he arrived in Jerusalem. Through trickery and treachery, one of his disciples, Judas, led the authorities to his resting place, and he was arrested and crucified. His disciples fled at first, and many had their hopes dashed.

But three days later, the disciples regrouped, convinced that Jesus had risen from the dead. This, they believed, had proclaimed him as 'Lord' and 'Messiah'.

Jesus of History/Christ of Faith?

The Gospels see Jesus through the lens of the resurrection; everything he said and did was reinterpreted through this belief. Scholars debate how much is original to Jesus.

The German scholar Rudolf Bultmann (1884–1976) was sceptical about almost everything in the Gospels, apart from the story of Jesus dying on a cross. He argued that the early church had no interest in what the actual Jesus of history had said and done; it was the risen Christ they cared about, the Christ of faith. More conservative scholars point out that if they are not the same man or being, then Christian faith is an illusion. There must be a link.

Some have applied strict tests to ascertain what might be original to Jesus. They note constant themes, such as his inclusion of social outcasts, and how some of his sayings present original ideas unknown in the Judaism of his day, and which were ignored by the church. (But a Jesus who agreed with nothing in Judaism

> *Moreover, a calculated deception should have produced greater unanimity. Instead there seem to have been competitors: 'I saw him first!' 'No! I did!'… That Jesus' followers (and later Paul) had resurrection experiences is, in my judgment, a fact. What the reality was that gave rise to the experiences I do not know…*
>
> E.P. SANDERS,
> *THE HISTORICAL FIGURE OF JESUS*

or the church that came after him would be an odd figure, indeed!) Others are more careful still, stressing the role of oral transmission in the culture, and the skill people possessed to do this. Many scholars now recognize more primitive tradition and a substantial historicity in the Gospels, even if material has been interpreted and reworked.

Risen?

Scholars have different assessments of the resurrection stories. These involve three elements: an empty tomb;

> *A well-trained pupil is like a well-plastered cistern that loses not a drop.*
>
> RABBI EPHRAIM

The Resurrection by Matthias Grünewald (c. 1475–1528) emphasizes the event as a transformation into spiritual glory, and not just a corpse being revived.

1 Corinthians 15:3–6). However, visions and feelings of new life are mentioned. The epistles (letters from the apostles) were written before the Gospels – is the empty tomb a later exaggeration of an earlier, spiritual experience, or do the Gospels record a primitive tradition here? More conservative scholars allow for the empty tomb. They point out that the empty-tomb tradition is in all four Gospels. If the body of Jesus rose too, though, then it was not a crudely physical event. The physical was transformed, taken up into glory. It was not left to rot. Others believe passionately in a spiritual rising, but are agnostic about what happened to the physical body.

We can never ascertain exactly what happened by historical enquiry alone. The fact is that the disciples did change. They were a dispirited, frightened bunch, hiding away. They emerged galvanized, preached in the face of death threats, and launched a vital, new religion upon the ancient world.

The Resurrection by Matthias Grünewald (c. 1475–1528) emphasizes the event as a transformation into spiritual glory, and not just a corpse being revived.

visions of the risen Christ; and a change in the frightened disciples.

Despite differences and small contradictions, these three elements are there in all four accounts in the Gospels. It is interesting, though, that while all four Gospels have the empty-tomb story, this is not mentioned elsewhere in the New Testament (though it might seem to be assumed:

The Man and the Myth

Myths are stories about important matters and universal themes. They are an insight into our inner selves. The story of Jesus is often assumed to be akin to ancient myths, with its central role for a dying and rising deity.

Pagan religions knew of the birth of divine saviours. The cult of Isis, for example, originated in ancient Egypt, where she was called 'Mother of God' (*Mut Netjer*), in the 2nd millennium BCE. She was shown nursing her son, Horus, the divine saviour, who had avenged his father, Osiris. Osiris had been killed by his brother, Seth, and then revived again by Isis. Images of Isis and Horus and similar female deities influenced early Christian artwork of the Virgin Mary and the infant Jesus.

Dying and rising gods were also aplenty, such as Osiris and Dionysus. H.G. Wells, in his *History of the World*, assumed that the idea of the resurrection was just a borrowing of the old vegetation myths, as a

Late-Egyptian sculpture of Isis nursing her son, Horus. Such images influenced early Christian depictions of the Madonna and child.

wandering Jewish holy man was made into a corn king in the popular, pagan imagination.

A real man in real time

Some believers point out that if there were no mythological features in the Gospels, then something would be wrong. If myth deals with universals, such as the struggle between light and darkness, then the Jesus story must be imbued with them. Otherwise, it is just a little, local Jewish story. The Gospel writers set the details of his life against a sense of cosmic battle. Furthermore, Jesus was a real man in history, who was executed when Tiberius was the Roman emperor and Pontius Pilate was the Roman prefect of Judea. There are scattered references to Jesus

Pagan images of mother goddesses and their child may have influenced Christian art, but the Jesus story is based upon a real man, not a mythical being. *Madonna del Granduca* by Raphael (1483–1520).

C.S. Lewis was a convinced atheist until a study of the classics and of myth began his soul-searching. He was converted to faith in Christ, and said his moment of decision was like stepping out of a suit of armour.

> *Christ, who was executed
> by sentence of the procurator
> Pontius Pilate in the reign
> of Tiberius.*
>
> CORNELIUS TACITUS,
> *THE ANNALS*, c. 112 CE

as an actual man in history in Roman and Jewish writings of the time. This is not a mythical hero from never-never land. Classical myths spoke of eternal events. The stories never actually happened, but the state they describe (life coming out of the death of winter) is

> *God is more than a god, not less;
> Christ is more than Balder, not
> less. We must not be ashamed of
> the mythical radiance resting on
> our theology. We must not be
> nervous about 'parallels' and
> 'pagan Christs': they ought to be
> there — it would be a stumbling
> block if they weren't...*
>
> C.S. LEWIS,
> *MYTH BECOME FACT*

constant. The Jesus story was about time past, a particular man in a particular age, but with a message for all time. C.S. Lewis argued that all the pagan myths of dying and rising gods were good dreams sent to humanity to prepare for the coming of Christ. Christ was a corn king, but one made flesh.

The Gospel Spreads

The twelve disciples started more than they knew; the gospel of Jesus spread rapidly throughout the Roman empire.

The Christian faith spread from port to port, from city to city, along established trade routes, as the disciples and other preachers travelled widely with their itinerant ministries. One New Testament document, the Acts of the Apostles, describes some of this process. It collects various stories, some very early and primitive, and some claiming to use eyewitness reports. It mentions many accurate historical details in passing, such as the names of minor officials, who are attested by archaeological remains. We do not know what happened to some of the other early leaders. Legends tell us that Peter ended up in Rome, Mark in Egypt and Thomas in India.

The starting point in e ach new centre was the local Jewish synagogue. The earliest Christianity was a variant form of Judaism. Reactions varied – sometimes the preachers were rejected, sometimes people listened. Each synagogue had a group of Gentile supporters known as 'God-fearers', who

This is my blood of the covenant, which is poured out for many.

JESUS, AT THE LAST SUPPER, MARK 14:24

sought to worship one God, but stopped short of becoming Jews. The food laws and circumcision were some reasons for their hesitation; the gospel allowed them to belong without these

Ruins of the 4th-century synagogue in Capernaum. This replaced the synagogue that Jesus taught at during his ministry.

rituals. The early Christian communities took in large numbers of Gentile converts, and the two faiths eventually divided. This was accelerated by the fall of Jerusalem in 70 CE and a Jewish council in 84 CE which rejected Christianity as a valid part of Judaism.

'Suddenly a light from heaven flashed around him' (Acts 9:3). *The Conversion of Paul* by Schiavone (1522–63).

PAUL THE APOSTLE

Paul of Tarsus was a leading missionary and preacher. After being bitterly opposed to the Christians, he had a dramatic conversion experience on the way to Damascus. He seems to have been an overly zealous and scrupulous Pharisee, who found real forgiveness and acceptance through his new faith in Christ. He understood the Gentile mind and adapted the message accordingly, while trying to stay faithful to his Jewish roots. He taught a doctrine of grace – unmerited favour – through the blood of Christ. The death of Christ was understood as an atonement sacrifice, a super-powerful version of the offerings of animals and their blood in the temple. This made these earlier offerings redundant, for forgiveness could now come through what Christ had done alone, and the Holy Spirit could live within the believer. Ritual food laws and circumcision were not necessary for Gentile converts, as they could know Christ's forgiveness through the cross alone.

Traces of this can be seen in other New Testament writings, such as the account of the Last Supper, but they present other models of salvation too. On the cross Jesus defeated the powers of evil, or showed a wonderful example of love in action.

The kingdom teaching also took on a new slant; Jesus was to return at the end of the age. There were striking and poetic ideas about this, and also a sense that the kingdom can begin within the believer's heart, now: 'Christ has died, Christ is risen, Christ will come again.'

71

'In This Sign Conquer…'

Christianity was legalized by the emperor Constantine in the 4th century CE, and it later became the official religion of the empire, after years of suspicion and sporadic persecution.

The Jews had been given the freedom not to worship the emperor, but Gentile converts to Christianity posed a new problem. With Christianity increasingly separate from official Judaism, Christians were accused of treason, and sometimes forced to sacrifice to Caesar. Persecutions were occasional, depending upon the attitude of the emperor or the local officials. There were many years when Christians were left in peace and the faith gradually grew. They did not always

The Chi-Rho comprises the first two letters (X and P) of the Greek word for Christ. Silver plaque from the 4th century CE.

THE MARTYRS

There are numerous tales of Christians who were beheaded or given to the lions. Polycarp was put to death in 155 CE. He refused to sacrifice to the emperor, saying, 'Eighty and six years have I served him, and he has done me no wrong. How then can I blaspheme my Lord and Saviour?'

These were brave and holy people without a doubt, but the early church seemed to develop something of a martyr complex. It was one thing to give your life if you had to, but quite another to go looking for martyrdom. Even after the church was at peace and tolerated, many turned to monasticism as an alternative to martyrdom. An unhealthy asceticism and loathing of the earth took root, which was far from the life-loving and celebrating figure of Jesus. Some think that this complex also produced an aggression towards those who did not agree, and fuelled the fires of schisms and condemnations for 'heresy' in later times. It might have all been different if the Romans had been more content to 'live and let live', or if the gospel had spread east into Hindu, Buddhist and Taoist areas.

Emperor Constantine granted toleration to Christians, but he probably remained a sun-worshipper until near the end of his life – he only accepted baptism on his deathbed.

Later church buildings followed the layout of the Roman house, with the courtyard and the table area for eating 'al fresco'. Larger churches followed the layout of the Roman basilica, the town hall, which had a hall and table area for the officials.

meet in secret in houses or in the Roman catacombs – burial chambers where communion services were held at the graves of martyrs who had died for the faith. In later years, houses were converted into church centres, with a hall for the celebration of the eucharist, the thanksgiving meal of bread and wine, rooms for teaching and a baptistry. People in those days were often immersed in a tank, or stood in a pool while water was poured over them.

Constantine

Constantine was proclaimed emperor by his troops at York in 306 CE. He was a sun-worshipper, as were many in the army. At his prayers before crossing to take control of Rome, legend has it that he saw a vision in the sky as the sun was rising. This was the Christian 'Chi-Rho' symbol, with the words *'In hoc signo vinces'* ('In this sign you shall conquer'). Constantine legalized Christianity in 313 CE with the Edict of Milan, and he used the Chi-Rho on his military standards. He also moved his capital from Rome to the eastern city of Byzantium, renaming it Constantinople (now Istanbul). Christians had their taxes reduced, but the old faiths could carry on. This began to change in 380 CE with the emperor Theodosius. He declared the old ways demented and foolish, and before long, they died out.

Throughout the world a bright and glorious day, an unclouded brilliance, illuminated all the churches of Christ with a heavenly light.

BISHOP EUSEBIUS, WRITING ABOUT CONSTANTINE'S CONVERSION

Emperor Constantine with his mother Helena. Sixteenth-century fresco from Sucevita Monastery, Romania.

Christendom

Christianity as an established religion permeated Western and Eastern culture for many years, though this was often very nominal and misunderstandings led to schism.

Rome fell in the west to advancing Germanic tribes in 410 CE, and the last emperor abdicated in 476 CE. Emperors continued leading the Byzantine empire in the East from Constantinople until 1453. The Western church looked more and more to the pope in Rome, the bishop who ruled in Peter's city and could claim a succession from him. The pope was always a 'first among equals', being respected by all the bishops, but there was a gradual elevation and centralization of his power, which the Eastern churches found increasingly hard to tolerate. One pope, Leo III, attempted to restore the Roman empire in the West when he crowned Charlemagne king of the Franks in St Peter's Church in 800 CE. Charlemagne was

Bust reliquary of the emperor Charlemagne from 1349.

hailed as the new Augustus and known as the Holy Roman Emperor. This title was passed down for many years, but the Holy Roman Emperor never quite succeeded in unifying the emerging nation states of Europe into anything like an empire.

East and West

The second major schism came in 1054. A papal representative, a legate, excommunicated the patriarch of Constantinople, the principal bishop in the Byzantine empire. The patriarch issued a series of

If in this city you ask anyone for change, he will discuss with you whether God the Son is begotten or unbegotten. If you ask about the quality of bread, you will receive the answer that 'God the father is greater, God the Son is less.'

A 4TH-CENTURY BISHOP,
SPEAKING OF CONSTANTINOPLE

Images of Christos Pantocrator, the ruler of all, appeared on domed ceilings of Eastern churches after the empire embraced Christianity. Christ was portrayed as a heavenly emperor – a far cry from the man from Nazareth. Byzantine mosaic (c. 1150) from Cappella Palatina, Sicily.

anathemas (severe, rejecting criticisms) against the legate. The pope neither confirmed nor denied the excommunication. This came after a series of tensions and disputes over his authority and some divergent practices (such as allowing priests to marry). Crusaders attacked Constantinople in 1204, causing great distress, and this pushed the two churches even further apart. This was a huge travesty of Christian fellowship.

EARLY SCHISMS

The first major splits between the churches came in the 5th century CE. This was over the understanding of the nature and person of Christ, a fine-tuning of doctrine that used specialized terms not present in the Bible or the earliest writings. People used words that did not always have the same meaning across the empire, and they easily misunderstood each other. Political groupings and intrigues did not help matters, and mutual condemnations flowed. Churches such as the Copts, the Ethiopians and the Syrians embraced a position known as monophysite ('one nature'), which was taken to mean that Christ was only God and not really human; in fact, it said that he was one person, God and man joined in one. Others, such as the Nestorians, claimed

to have been misunderstood. Nestorius (died c. 451 CE), a monk from Antioch, was condemned by the Council of Ephesus in 431. It was feared that he taught that God and man were not fully united in Christ. To flee persecution, the Nestorians turned east, moving into the Persian empire and beyond. Nestorian communities were discovered in the 13th century by Marco Polo on his travels. It is only since the latter part of the 20th century that these ancient oriental churches have entered into dialogue with the Orthodox churches.

Renaissance and Reformation

The Western church kept much of the old learning intact, through the role of the monasteries with their scholars, scribes and libraries. Though the Roman empire had gone, learning continued throughout the 'Dark Ages'. New learning and reform movements caused intellectual and social upheavals.

Monks and nuns lived separatist and cloistered lives, but also ran the earliest forms of hospitals. Friars were able to wander freely and became orders of preachers. Francis of Assisi (1181/2–1226) is the most famous, a man who gave up everything for the love of God, and who could calm the wild animals by his prayers.

The Scholastics, or Schoolmen, were prominent from the 13th century, monk scholars who studied the ancient Greek texts of philosophers such as Aristotle. There had been various earlier thinkers who had used aspects of Greek philosophy to explain Christian teachings, such as Augustine of Hippo (354–430), a convert from pagan cults. He used Plato's division of the soul into mind/will and reason to explain the Trinity. Others used terms from Greek thought (*hypostasis/prosopon* – 'substance/person') to show how God was one thing and

yet three, and the *logos* idea in the opening chapter of John's Gospel (where it is translated as 'Word') used a common philosophical term of that culture. Some of the Greek writings, translated into Arabic by Muslim scholars, had been rediscovered through trade with the Muslim world. New ideas and inventions were coming into Europe, and this led to a rebirth of learning, the Renaissance, with effects on literature, art and science. The most famous of the Scholastics was Thomas Aquinas (c. 1225–74), a Dominican friar. He brought Aristotelian concepts into theology that became unquestionable for many years.

The Reformers

The 16th-century Reformation followed on from the revival of learning in the Renaissance and the rise of humanism (an interest in the development of human knowledge and science, and a tolerant, open attitude to ideas). Humanist scholars, such as Desiderius Erasmus (1469–1536), satirized the hypocrisy of the medieval church. The Reformers sought to restore the church to biblical principles.

The political situation was relevant too, with emerging nation states and princes eager to strike out in independence from the pope or Holy Roman Emperor. The German princes welcomed the Reformed faith,

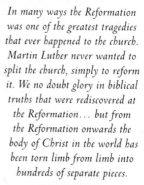

In many ways the Reformation was one of the greatest tragedies that ever happened to the church. Martin Luther never wanted to split the church, simply to reform it. We no doubt glory in biblical truths that were rediscovered at the Reformation… but from the Reformation onwards the body of Christ in the world has been torn limb from limb into hundreds of separate pieces.

DAVID WATSON,
I BELIEVE IN THE CHURCH

KEY REFORMERS

Martin Luther (1483–1546), an Augustinian monk, became a professor of scripture at the newly formed University of Wittenberg, Germany. He broke with Rome in 1520.

John Calvin (1509–64) was a French priest who broke with Rome in 1533, believing that he was called to help restore the church to its original purity. He fled to Switzerland and settled at Geneva, leading the Reformed Church there.

Ulrich Zwingli (1484–1531) was a Swiss priest based in Zürich. He effectively broke with Rome in 1522.

Martin Luther. Woodcut after Lucas Cranach.

as this allowed them a new freedom. In England, politics also played its part. King Henry VIII separated from the pope to secure a divorce, but he kept the actual worship of the church along Roman Catholic lines for much of his reign. Archbishop Cranmer introduced Reformed ideas later, producing the first two English Prayer Books of 1549 and 1552.

Moves to Unity

The 20th century saw the rise of the ecumenical movement, which strove to draw the different Christian churches closer together. Modern renewal movements have also stressed this unity.

The lack of toleration and the inability to listen have marred the church of Christ down through the ages. Power play and politics have also muddied the waters. The Eastern Orthodox churches separated over disputes about the person of Christ; East split from West under clouds of mutual condemnation; and the Western church imploded in various schisms at the Reformation. Believers of different stripes were imprisoned, beaten, tortured or executed for their stance; Christian has hurt and killed fellow Christian. This hatred of difference and the shedding of blood has fostered a disillusionment with the organized church in the modern age, and it has contributed to the rise of secularism and atheism.

Moves to unity began slowly in the late 19th century, and the impetus gathered momentum between the wars. The Second World War finally convinced people that there would be no peace in Europe without peace

Whoever drinks the water I give him will never thirst. Indeed, the water I give him will become in him a spring of water welling up to eternal life.
JESUS, JOHN 4:14

between the churches. The World Council of Churches was set up in 1948. It has over 300 member churches from over 100 different countries. Its slogan is 'All One in Christ'. At more local or national levels, churches encourage joint worship, mission and teaching where possible. Local prayer groups and study groups happily mix different denominations together in ways that would have been unthinkable some years ago.

Renewal in the Spirit
The New Testament speaks of a personal renewal and blessing

The Roman Catholic Church underwent a major reform in the 1960s at the Second Vatican Council, which embraced ecumenism as a divine duty and command.

If the churches are reconciled, then the world will come running as to a mother.
BROTHER ROGER OF TAIZÉ

Charismatic worship in a church in Colombia.

by the Holy Spirit. This experience has always been around in the church, but has been manifested much more widely in the 20th century, spreading to the mainline denominations. This has helped to bring different types of Christians together for prayer and praise who sense an amazing oneness in the Spirit.

A Christlike God?

Jesus lived and taught the love of God; this man of compassion revealed a God who was ready to forgive and welcome the wayward back into his kingdom. It was a radical message, based upon grace and not human effort. God is Christlike. For too many, God has been a Cosmic Judge from whom they keep their distance; Jesus dared to call him 'Abba, Father'. Christians have hurt each other and have betrayed the message of Christ. Love stands out and beckons us to follow in the life of Jesus. If the churches learn to love one another, what power and healing might be released into the world?

Summing up

Jesus of Nazareth started a radical revolution in spirituality from provincial, peasant roots that spread throughout the Roman empire and beyond. With the eventual conversion of the Roman emperors, the church of the marginalized became more state-sanctioning and less prophetic. 'Christendom' was born, a system of church–state government that influenced thought and spawned great theology and philosophy for many years. Changes in society have seen a return to the roots, as Christianity is sought and practised more and more by those seeking the original vision of a radical spiritual life and experience.

THE MUSLIM WORLD

Islam is the faith practised by a Muslim. The same Arabic word lies behind these two words: *slm*, meaning 'peace' or 'submission'. A Muslim is one who submits to the will of God and therefore finds peace. Though the Prophet Muhammad began preaching this faith in Arabia in the 6th century CE, Muslims believe that their faith is an ancient one, being, in essence, exactly the same as that of Jesus and the prophets before him who are mentioned in the Hebrew scriptures, right back to Adam himself. They think that the Jews and the Christians ('People of the Book') to whom revelation also came, have distorted their scriptures and gone astray on some points.

Muslims believe that they are

The annual pilgrimage to Mecca, when thousands of Muslims converge from all over the world.

guided to the straight or right path in life as they pray and obey God. The first sura (chapter) of their holy book, the Qur'an, mentions this. Muslims recite this sura as they begin their formal prayers.

The new religious movement united the warring Arab tribes and introduced monotheism to large areas of the world. The new faith influenced learning and scientific knowledge – great advances in medicine were made in Islamic society, for example. The Muslims kept the ancient learning of the Greeks alive when Europe was plunged into the Dark Ages. Despite many similarities between Islam and Christianity, the two faiths have sometimes struggled for supremacy, and the Crusades have left a legacy of mistrust to this day.

Contents

In the name of Allah, Most Gracious, Most Merciful.
Praise be to Allah, the Cherisher and Sustainer of the Worlds;
Most Gracious, Most Merciful;
Master of the Day of Judgment.
Thee do we worship and thine aid we seek.
Show us the straight way.
The way of those on whom thou has bestowed thy grace, those whose (portion) is not wrath, and who go not astray.

QUR'AN, SURA I

The Prophet

Muhammad said that he experienced dramatic visions and messages given through the mediation of the angel Gabriel. He recited these and they formed the text of the Qur'an.

Muhammad (c. 570–632) was a seeker, a devout soul who would withdraw into the desert and meditate in a cave on Mount Hira. On his travels, he would have met Jews and Christians and listened to their stories and ideas. Christian monks living in desert communities seemed to have made a particular impression on him with their sincerity, simplicity and devotion. The Arabs knew of wandering seers, the *hanifs*, who covered their heads with their cloaks, and uttered wisdom and insights from the gods. The Arab tribes were polytheists, with two chief deities, Allah and Allat ('the God' and 'the Goddess'). Their sacred building was in Mecca: the Ka'aba. This ancient, cube-like structure housed many statues and icons from the different gods around them. Muslims believe that this building was first erected by the prophet Abraham, and dedicated to the worship of the one God. It was to become the holiest shrine of Islam, and the focus of the yearly pilgrimage, the hajj.

This was Muhammad's background, but he did not expect what happened in his fortieth year on the 'night of power'. In the month of Ramadan, the 27th day, in 611 CE, he heard a commanding voice saying, 'Recite!' and he

Muhammad claimed to have had a miraculous night journey to Jerusalem in the twinkling of an eye. There he ascended through the seven heavens and met previous prophets. As he spoke with Allah in the vision, it was agreed that Muslims would offer prayer five times per day.

MUHAMMAD'S EARLY LIFE

Muhammad was born in 570 CE after his father had died, and was at first looked after by a foster mother, Halima. His real mother died when he was six. He then went to live with his grandfather, who died two years later. Muhammad was then looked after by his uncle, Abu Talib. He was poor, and the young Muhammad had to earn a living as a shepherd, not being trained to read or write. Later, he worked as a trader with his uncle. Trade routes passed through Mecca and brought many travellers and their goods – as well as their ideas.

Muhammad prospered as he entered the service of a wealthy widow, Khadija, whom he later married.

Muhammad's night ride, surrounded by angels. Many Muslims would not now depict angels for fear that people might worship them. 17th-century Persian miniature.

realized that he was in the presence of a great and holy power, later understood as the angel Gabriel. He was shown a cloth with Arabic words, and, by a miracle, could recite them. This left Muhammad frightened and disturbed until his wife comforted him.

*Proclaim! (or read!) in the name of thy Lord
and Cherisher, who created –
Created man, out of a (mere) clot of congealed blood:
Proclaim! And Thy Lord is Most Bountiful –
He who taught (the use of) the Pen –
Taught man what he knew not...*

QUR'AN, SURA 96:1–5

Months later, he had a vision again and this convinced him of his prophetic calling.

Mecca

Muhammad began to preach in Mecca, and he faced opposition from the ruling tribe, who feared that their trade would suffer if people embraced this new faith and the idols of local gods were destroyed. Some early Muslims were persecuted and tortured, being martyred for their faith. Muhammad urged many to flee to safety.

Muhammad fled to Yathrib, later called Medina, in 622. The leaders of Mecca tried to attack Medina, but they were defeated in 624. Eventually, Muhammad led his followers to Mecca and took control of it in 630. The elders stood before Muhammad, expecting cruel treatment and death. Muhammad offered forgiveness: 'Go in peace. I say to you as Joseph said to his brothers, "There shall be no responsibility on you today. You are free."'

Muhammad died a year later and is buried in Medina.

Christians and Muslims

The early days of the Muslim empire saw a courteous and generous coexistence between the two faiths; the Crusades left a dreadful legacy of suspicion and betrayal.

The Qur'an teaches that there must be no compulsion in religion (sura 2:256). Christians are to be treated courteously for they are followers of the gospel, even if Muslims believe that this has been distorted. Great reverence is shown to 'Jesus the son of Mary' ('Isa ibn Maryam') in Islam, and there are many sayings attributed to him in the Hadith. However, Muslims reject any idea of his divinity.

When areas such as Egypt and Syria fell to the Muslims, the Christian communities felt that their new leaders were no better or worse than the old ones; they had been taxed and sometimes persecuted by

Lit is such a light in houses, which Allah hath permitted to be raised to honour; for the celebration, in them, of his name: in them is he glorified in the mornings and in the evenings, again and again.

QUR'AN, SURA 24:36

Fourteenth-century manuscript illumination of the First Crusade, showing templar knights in front of Jerusalem, while the Saracens are inside.

THE CRUSADES

Jerusalem fell to Caliph Umar in 638 CE. He was greeted by Patriarch Sophronius and escorted around the Church of the Holy Sepulchre. It was time for the Muslim midday prayers, and the patriarch invited him to say them there. Umar refused, saying that this would be taken as a sign that he had claimed this church for Islam. He went outside to say them. How different matters were when the Christian Crusaders retook Jerusalem in 1099. Muslims, Jews and non-Orthodox Christians were massacred in the streets. The area around the temple mount was said to have run knee-deep in blood.

> *He (Jesus) said, I am
> indeed a servant of Allah: He
> hath given me revelation and
> made me a prophet. And He hath
> made me blessed wheresoever I be,
> and hath enjoined on me Prayer
> and Charity as long as I live.*
>
> QUR'AN, SURA 19:30–31

the Byzantines. Many of the Christians in these areas were monophysites. In some cases, they had a greater freedom to worship, although all Christian men had to pay a tax. Churches and monasteries were not to be touched, and the Eastern monks had such an impact upon Muhammad that they might have an indirect mention in the Qur'an. A lyrical passage about the light of Allah probably refers to these holy men praying in their churches and communities. The prayer positions of some Eastern Christians – bowing low and prostrating oneself on the ground – influenced the salat prayers of Muslims, which are performed five times a day.

The future

The West, and many in the churches, tend to see Islam as 'the Other', and a troublesome one at that. What is to be made of a movement that claims a prophet for which the church has no use? It was once the custom to see Muhammad as possessed, deluded or fanatical. This is not true to the sources. He was a genuine, searching, holy man who brought monotheism to many people, and there is much in common between the two ancient faiths. Dialogue needs to continue, and many misunderstandings can be cleared up. There are real differences, particularly over the person of Jesus, but the majority hope that toleration and respect will eventually triumph.

Church of the Holy Sepulchre in Jerusalem.

85

Struggle and Gain

Islam spread through Arabia and the Near East, eventually taking over the Byzantine empire. The initial expansion was due to a mixture of self-defence and the oppressive corruption of neighbouring powers.

Muhammad had managed to unite the warring Arab tribes behind him, and his successors faced threats from Persia and the Byzantine empire based in Constantinople. Abu Bakr, Muhammad's close acquaintance, was chosen as his successor, or caliph. Abu Bakr died two years later, having nominated Umar ibn al-Khattab as the next caliph. Caliph Umar ruled for ten years (634–44), and he proposed that an electoral council should be set up to decide on his successor. The council proposed two men – Uthman ibn Affan and Ali ibn Talib, a cousin of Muhammad. The community was divided, but Uthman was eventually elected as the new caliph, only to be murdered in 656 CE. Ali succeeded him, but various divisions were now at work within the Muslim society. Ali was killed in 661. This ended the reign of the 'four rightly guided caliphs', as they became known; unelected rulers were to replace them in the future. In the period of their reign, Islam had spread rapidly.

> If I do any good, give me your support. If I do any wrong, set me right… Obey me as long as I obey Allah and his messenger. If I disobey Allah and his messenger, you are free to disobey me.

FROM ABU BAKR'S SPEECH UPON BEING CHOSEN AS CALIPH

Muslim warrior on a camel, from an Arab manuscript, 12th century.

'The supreme jihad is against oneself.'

> *To those against whom war is made, permission is given (to fight) because they are wronged.*
>
> QUR'AN, SURA 22:39

A major split came after the death of Ali. Some rebelled and supported Ali's son, Husayn. Caliph Yazid surrounded Husayn's supporters and massacred them at the battle of Karbala in 680. Their subsequent followers became the Shia. Shia Islam believes in the imams, who are descended from Muhammad, Ali being the first. Most Muslims are Sunni, who follow the early caliphs and do not recognize those after Ali.

Rapid expansion

Abu Bakr sent an ambassador to Constantinople, but the Byzantine emperor tried to overthrow the Muslims. City after city fell to the new movement, and they took control of Egypt, Syria and North Africa, seriously weakening the Byzantine empire.

By the end of Umar's reign, Muslim rule spread from Gujarat in India to Libya in North Africa. Emperor Yazdegird III of Persia sought help from China and other neighbours, but the Muslims decisively defeated his armies in 642. Uthman entered Spain and made inroads into China. Half of the known world came under Muslim rule. The Byzantine empire eventually fell in 1453. Tribes had been taxed to fund the Byzantine wars, and this had fostered their resentment. The invaders were welcomed.

JIHAD

Jihad means 'struggle'. This can be an inner, personal struggle against sin, or a social struggle against injustice. It can also involve taking up arms in self-defence. It is not meant to be a war of aggression to lay territorial claims or to impose a new order or faith on a nation. It has to follow certain rules of conduct, such as not harming women, children and unarmed civilians; places of worship must be left untouched; property should not be destroyed, and the environment must not be damaged. Clearly, fanatical terrorist attacks using bombs in pizza restaurants, or hijacking airliners are outside these rules and cannot be classed as acts of jihad. Jihad is a form of 'just war'. Muhammad once stated, 'The supreme jihad is against oneself.'

The Muslim Civilization

The stability and prosperity of the Muslim world, coupled with intrinsic values — seeking knowledge and serving humanity — led to intellectual growth and a wealth of new discoveries.

The Abbasid Caliphate, based in Baghdad, began in 750 CE and lasted for five centuries until 1258. These rulers stressed justice and fairness in government and business, and were passionate about learning. A whole knowledge industry blossomed. Islam had certain implicit values, which were drawn out and made explicit. These are *khalifa*, *adl* and *ilm*:

◆ *Khalifa* means 'stewardship' or 'trusteeship' over the earth and its resources.
◆ *Adl* means 'justice', and Muslim scholars feel that the main motive of revelation and guidance is to establish justice on earth.
◆ *Ilm* means 'knowledge'. Knowledge is necessary to understand the environment and to bring about justice. The opening words of the Qur'an — 'Recite' or 'Read' — have been taken as a command to do just that to God's creation. It is a religious and moral duty to seek to understand the world.

Books and writing

The quest for knowledge led to the translation of many texts from the ancient world

The central court of Al-Azhar Mosque, Cairo, Egypt, which became a university in 988 CE.

A whole industry grew around the need to make rapid copies of books, and the *warraqeen* ('copyists'; 'those who handle paper') could produce a few hundred pages within hours. They made their own paper, held stalls in markets, and organized libraries and bookshops.

(including the Greek philosophers) and from neighbouring countries, such as Sanskrit texts from India. This wealth of written material was unparalleled. After translation came critique and a sifting of ideas to comment upon these from an Islamic perspective. This led to the development of books and the use of paper, taken from the Chinese. Paper was thinner than parchment and allowed books to be made more easily.

Colleges and universities

The mosque, as the place of gathering for worship, was the original centre for learning. As the knowledge industry grew, larger areas were needed. These took the form of the *madrassah* ('college'), with a shaikh ('professor') in charge. He would sit on a low chair surrounded by his students, and his assistants would be 'readers' who would literally have to read out texts. To this day, Western universities have a 'chair' in each subject area, which is held by a reader or professor.

The *jamnia* ('university') began in Cairo at Al-Azhar in 970 CE. As well as religion, students studied logic, philosophy, mathematics, physics and astronomy.

Law and Interpretation

Muslim concepts of law and the interpretation of their traditions were very creative and open until the decline of Muslim civilization at the end of the 14th century.

The sharia, meaning 'path to a watering hole', is the body of traditions, values and ideals that guide the formation of Muslim law. These are derived from the Qur'an, the Sunna (life and sayings of Muhammad contained in the Hadith) and *ijma* ('the consensus of the community'). Analogous reasoning also comes into play as scholars try to apply general principles to particular circumstances. Rather than slavishly following a set code, there was a growing, creative attempt to permeate the whole of life with principles faithful to Islam.

Fiqh

Fiqh means 'intelligence and knowledge'. It is Islamic jurisprudence, struggling to understand contemporary problems, and working out how to apply the faith to them. As such, it is not revelation, which is always unchanging, but a human construction that can be

At a traditional Afghan wedding, the women and men celebrate in separate areas, with music and dancing. Here, the women, wearing burkhas, play tambourines.

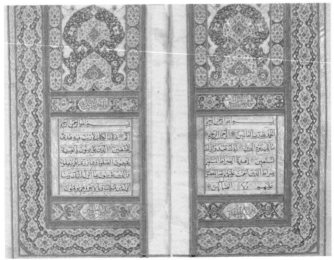

Illustration from a North Indian manuscript of the Qur'an from 1838.

WOMEN

The role of women illustrates the modern difficulties. The Qur'an gives only general advice about how people (men and women) should dress. How this is interpreted can vary from culture to culture; the burka of Taliban

Afghanistan is one extreme. Does the Qur'an even insist that all women should cover their head, and if so, with anything other than a scarf? Modern Muslims wish to return to the more open, general ethics of the Qur'an, and not specific, time-conditioned ways of understanding these.

The Qur'an grants equal rights to men and women. Women can divorce a man, but Islamic jurists over the centuries have effectively denied them this right. Contemporary Muslim women intellectuals stress how early Islam actually undermined patriarchy and held to a religious bond between men, women and their creator. They are beginning to challenge the gender bias of many Muslim writers and (purely social) traditions through the ages.

Say to the believing men that they should lower their gaze and guard their modesty... And say to the believing women that they should lower their gaze and guard their modesty... that they should draw their veils over their bosoms and not display their beauty except to their husbands...

QUR'AN, SURA 24:30–31

changed. The early jurists hated any idea that their advice could become ossified into a formal school of thought, but that is exactly what happened. The old rulings, or fatwas, became stuck in time, to be repeated for all ages, even if they no longer fit contemporary society.

Ijtihad

Ijtihad means striving as hard as possible to understand a situation and what new ideas might be needed. It is about a more open thinking and interpretation.

Sharia should work to establish justice between people as free individuals. It cannot be imposed by force, but needs to be freely chosen. A just society needs to be open to think and to seek new knowledge, to struggle with general principles and particular applications, with permanence and change. It needs to harness all resources possible to work for this aim. Thus, Muslims argue that they need to be free to influence their states by Islamic principles; Islamic 'fundamentalists', however, seek to force one set of interpretations upon a nation. They make the mistake of confusing sharia and *fiqh*.

Science and the Arts

The thirst for knowledge led to advances in scientific thinking and practice. The fundamentals of the modern scientific method with its experimentation and observation were laid centuries before thinkers such as Bacon, Galileo and Descartes were active in Europe.

Old laboratory reports demonstrating the establishment of the scientific method exist from 10th and 11th-century CE scientists. Logarithms and algebra were invented even earlier, by al-Khwarizmi in the 9th century CE. The name 'algebra' comes from his book, *Kitab al-jbr wa' muqabala* (*The Book of Inheritance*). Al-Battani also measured the circumference of the earth, and was only 24 seconds out in the measurement of the solar year.

Ibn al-Haytham worked in the 11th century CE with optics and lenses, establishing the laws of refraction and the fact that the eye reflects rays of sunlight, and does not actually emit them as had been believed. His *Optical Thesaurus* guided many Western thinkers in later years.

Chemistry developed, and paint was introduced for commercial use in the 10th century CE by Jabbir ibn Hayyan.

Manuals of surgery were written, hospitals were established in Muslim cities with separate wards for men and women, contagious diseases such as tuberculosis and smallpox

The astronomer Takiuddin in his observatory at Galata, 1581, showing astronomical instruments in use at the time. After an illuminated manuscript.

began to be recognized, midwifery was established, and ibn Nafis described the circulation of the blood in the 13th century – long before William Harvey in the 17th century.

Art

Muslim art centred around calligraphy and the depiction of Qur'anic verses, and extended to the decoration of pottery and tiles, as well as textile work, especially carpet weaving. Music was seen as a science because of its links with mathematics. Ideas of measured song and harmony were introduced to the West from Muslim practice, as well as a wide range of stringed instruments.

Students travelled to Muslim cities from all over Europe to learn from the masters of different subjects. Gradually, this new learning led to the European Renaissance.

Decline

Internal feuds and corrupt leadership led to the decline of Muslim civilization. The fall of Baghdad to the Mongols in 1258, and then of Grenada to

I... travelled to China, Sri Lanka, Byzantium and Southern Russia...

IBN BATTULA,
A 14TH-CENTURY TRAVELLER

The rapid expansion of the Muslim empires and the quest for knowledge led to expeditions and guides for travellers. The seas were charted using latitude and longitude, and the first spherical map of the world was produced in 1154. A postal system was introduced as early as the 10th century, and epic adventures about seafaring, such as Sinbad the Sailor, were popular.

Stonepaste 'Golden Horn' bottle from the Ottoman period, about 1530 CE.

the king of Spain in 1492 weakened Muslim society, and many manuscripts were lost or destroyed. Beyond this, however, was an internal inertia that led to a freezing of learning and a fear of seeking new knowledge and understandings of the Qur'an. *Ilm* came to mean religious knowledge only. This was the work of the ulema, the theologians, who recommended a blind imitation and robbed Islam of its dynamism. The ulema resisted the introduction of the printing press for over 300 years – Europe took the Muslim inheritance and moved rapidly ahead. In time, this decline made Muslim lands ripe for conquest and colonization by Western powers.

Islam Today

Colonialism hastened the decline of Muslim civilization, but the roots go deeper. Modern movements to reverse this trend either seek to become more hardline, anti-Western and 'fundamentalist', or they are more creative and searching, seeking to return to the roots of the faith.

The colonial powers used a 'divide and rule' policy between princes and tribes. They also sought control over Islamic education. The Dutch, for example, closed the *madrassahs* in Indonesia when they took control in the 16th century, and only permitted primary education. Power structures were oppressive. The more subtle effects are in a world view of orientalism, whereby Islam is depicted as a part of a primitive culture that can be sexually louche and violent. Playing down or denying the earlier intellectual achievements of this great culture were also strategies of control.

Iranians brandish posters of the Ayatollah Khomeni during the Iranian revolution.

Reform and rebellion
Few armed uprisings against the colonial powers worked because of their greater strength and technology. Instead, Muslim thinkers tried to influence attitudes and revive the intellectual life of Islam. In the 18th century, al-Wahhab united the Arabian tribes and urged a return to the roots of Islam; his son, ibn Saud, gave his name to Saudi Arabia. In the 20th century, groups such as the Muslim Brotherhood in Egypt argued for political change, social justice and an Islamic state.

Creative thinking
Some Muslim thinkers wish to return to the early years of Islam, and to rediscover its communitarian, democratic and spiritual energy. Fundamentalism

is theocratic by imposition and moderates wish to see Islamic truth and values influence society instead: tradition needs to be rethought and freed from fossilization, the sharia needs to be rethought according to a new *fiqh*, looking at contemporary problems, and the faith needs a revived sense of *ijtihad*. New explorations and understandings of the Qur'an are invited.

FUNDAMENTALISM

The Iranian revolution of 1978–79 was hailed as a victory for Islam over Western forces, but its excesses disillusioned many Muslims. It denied the social conscience of Islam. For others, this began a demand for the establishment of Islamic states with a full return to traditional, sharia law. It is misleading to speak of Muslim 'fundamentalists', for all Muslims would say that they believe the Qur'an is the literal word of Allah. The term really describes political activists who seek to overthrow the West, and who wish to follow a strict interpretation of the sharia. The movement has arisen because people are angry and frustrated with what they see as Western indifference or oppression over the ages. They are also angry with their own past leaders, who have been too secularized and radical, often imprisoning traditionalists.

The future is to be lived.

Summing up

A new faith burst upon the world in 6th-century Arabia, seeing itself as the original faith of Abraham, which had been distorted by both the Jews and the Christians. Islam unified Arabian tribes, and it led to the establishment of an empire to rival those of Byzantium and Persia, bringing new discoveries, learning and science.

ENTERING THE MODERN WORLD

Greek philosophy was used by early Christian thinkers as a framework for developing Christian doctrine and ideas about the world. Augustine of Hippo (354–430) was the most prolific of these thinkers in the early centuries. Knowledge of the philosophers lived on in monasteries in the European Dark Ages, and then new manuscripts began to be discovered through trade with the Arab world early in the 2nd millennium. This revolutionized European thought

and brought Aristotle to the fore; Augustine had favoured Plato. The Roman empire looked to the deposit of Greek philosophy as the foundation of knowledge, and thus the early Christians sought to interpret and to develop the faith in this light. John's Gospel had used the term '*logos*', or 'Word', after all (John 1:1).

The Middle Ages had sought authority in the church, and in the writings of the Greek philosophers as a fixed body of knowledge that could not be questioned or bettered. There was a sense that all that could be known about the universe by human beings had been discovered; we must accept, humbly, the limitations of our abilities and our brains. The Scholastics were Christian theologians who studied the old philosophers and adapted their ideas to a Christian framework. They called Aristotle the Great Doctor, and the most influential of the Scholastics was Thomas Aquinas (1225–74).

The revival of learning that came with the rediscovery of the old philosophers began new enquiries that were to shake the foundations of the established order. New ideas took people into the 'modern' world.

Contents

Nothing is found in the intellect that has not been first in the senses.

THOMAS AQUINAS,
SUMMA THEOLOGICA

Thomas Aquinas

Aquinas sought to reconcile the thinking of Aristotle with Christian concepts, believing that reason and faith were separate routes to the same end.

Thomas Aquinas was born in Aquino to wealthy parents related to the king of France, and sent to be trained by the Benedictine monastery at Monte Cassino, where they had ambitions to make him abbot. He sought the intellectual life of the newly formed Dominican order of preachers, and he was imprisoned for 15 months by his family in an attempt to dissuade him. He joined the order in 1244, working in Paris and Rome, before settling in Naples to set up a new Dominican school, where he worked on his magnum opus, the *Summa Theologica*. Aquinas was introduced to the works of Aristotle while in Paris, and he adapted many of Aristotle's ideas. Aquinas held to a strict separation between reason and revelation, or faith, believing that the world could be understood by reason alone. Issues such as the creation, the resurrection and purgatory were matters of revealed faith that could not be deduced by reason alone, though they were

THE 'PROOFS' OF GOD'S EXISTENCE

Aquinas's proofs are more like theories or arguments. They are hardly beyond reasonable doubt. He accepted the earlier argument of Anselm of Canterbury (1033–1109), the ontological argument, whereby the idea of a Superior Being is an idea of perfection, and that to be perfect, it must exist in reality, beyond the world of ideas. He argued that this was beyond observation, as it depended upon intellectual realization alone. His classical proofs started with our existence in the world:

♦ The cosmological argument – what exists must have come from a First Cause or an Unmoved Mover; the cosmos demands a creator.
♦ The teleological argument – the cosmos has a purpose. This means both an ultimate purpose that we do not yet understand and an inbuilt order and sense of design. This purpose and design demand the existence of a creator.

Thomas Aquinas, shown here as a doctor of the church (meaning great teacher). This reveals how far he influenced the church in the Middle Ages.

not contrary to reason, and rational arguments could be given to uphold them. He also taught that any intellectual speculation had to begin with sense experience, as human beings were mental and physical beings. He worked out the classical philosophical 'proofs' for the existence of God with this in mind. He began with experience and deduced God's reality.

After his death, various rival orders and thinkers tried to criticize his theories, but the Dominicans accepted his views as their official stance, and his early canonization in 1323 led to his views becoming increasingly influential in the medieval church. Aquinas had opened up ideas that were to dominate and shape the world. Issues of the relation between sense experience and intellectual intuition, faith and reason, and the authority of the church were hotly debated in the centuries to come.

The Renaissance

The Renaissance was a widespread rebirth of learning that burst forth in the 14th century as old ideas and manuscripts were discovered.

The Renaissance came about after trade with the Muslim world brought Arabic texts and new knowledge across to the West. Muslim scholars had translated the works of Plato and Aristotle into Arabic, and their vocation to 'read' the

THE MEDIEVAL WORLD VIEW

Medieval society was worked out in a rigid hierarchy; God was in heaven, the angels were beneath him and the world rested at the centre of the universe, with the sun and the stars moving around it. Social organization followed suit: the king was on the throne, the nobles ruled in the castles, and the serfs worked the land for them.

The emergence of a free, merchant class who travelled widely and resided in cities shook this old order. New ideas and discoveries attacked the metaphysical underpinning, placing the sun at the centre of the universe, and raising new questions about faith and politics.

world and understand what they could led to new inventions and discoveries. Much of Western science is based upon their work. The Renaissance saw new realism in the arts, and developments in medicine, mathematics and architecture.

The Renaissance began in the independent city-states of Northern Italy. These were prosperous, and they sponsored philosophers, builders and artists. The rise of cities as the old feudal system broke down allowed a merchant class to

Giotto di Bondone (c. 1267–1337) was one of the first medieval artists to break with the conventions of two-dimensional Byzantine iconography. He painted more realistic figures and scenes, reflecting the humanist ideals of the time. *St Francis Gives His Coat to a Pauper*.

> *On how many charges am I not*
> *my own self-critic? Furthermore, if*
> *every type of man is included, it is*
> *clear that all vices are censured, not*
> *any individual. And so anyone*
> *who protests that he is injured*
> *betrays his own guilty conscience…*
>
> DESIDERIUS ERASMUS,
> *PRAISE OF FOLLY*

Desiderius Erasmus (1469–1536) dared to ridicule the cant and hypocrisy of the church more than most in his book, *Praise of Folly*. He had a healthy sense of the limitations of human wisdom, and he sought to bring people down to earth.

grow, which sought new trade routes and ways of making money.

Humanism

The emphasis upon human achievement and learning was known as 'humanism', in the sense of a celebration of the world and this life rather than speculations on the next. Old orders were being questioned, but with a firm belief in God and a fidelity to the church, even if the hypocrisy and corruption of the latter establishment were satirized. Scholars sought a more tolerant and honest church that embraced the glories of this world as well as the next.

Politics

Aristotle had argued that politics should work to

Erasmus Writing by Hans Holbein the Younger (1497–1543).

produce moral citizens, and the church sought to carry on this vision. Renaissance thinkers began to question the Great Doctor on a number of matters. Niccolò Machiavelli (1469–1527) fashioned *The Prince* upon the corrupt and ruthless Renaissance rulers he observed in Italy. He concluded that politics was about power and control of the people, arguing that morality and politics did not mix. This was the beginning of the idea of the secular state or civil society.

Not science as we know it…

Renaissance humanism was mixed with superstitions and magical ideas. Alchemy arose at this time as an esoteric science to discover secret, unifying and transforming principles in the elements. Natural events and objects were often believed to hold occult meanings. The shape of a plant could determine its use in medicine, for example.

The New Science

The 17th century saw the rise of a new way of knowing, which formed the foundations of modern science. The late 16th and early 17th centuries saw the work of thinkers such as Sir Francis Bacon in England and Galileo Galilei in Italy focused upon skills of observation.

Francis Bacon (1561–1626), while Lord Chancellor, in works such as *Advancement of Learning* in 1605, encouraged people to take Aristotle's ideas of induction seriously. Here, we learn from taking in information from the world around us, rather than deducing ideas within our minds. He sought to open up new ideas, rather than to slavishly follow traditional authorities. Trusting and using sense experience must rigorously question what the authorities tell us.

Tree of knowledge

Bacon described knowledge as being akin to a tree. There were three main branches, or faculties. These corresponded to the three faculties of the mind: memory, imagination and reason:

◆ Memory dealt with historical knowledge.
◆ Imagination dealt with poetry and the arts.
◆ Reason dealt with philosophy (which included what we now call the sciences).

Galileo

Galileo (1564–1642) modified the refracting telescope, which had been invented in the Netherlands in 1609. He used this to actually observe the

LEONARDO DA VINCI

Leonardo da Vinci (1452–1519) was a typical 'Renaissance man', with a wide-ranging knowledge of the arts and sciences. His notebooks are filled with sketches and designs for machines. None of these was made in his lifetime, but his was a visionary genius. He designed a tank – a vehicle with a wooden frame and four wheels, armed with four, small cannon. He sketched a parachute, made of rope and canvas. He drew a craft that was to be raised into the air by two rotating blades, similar to a helicopter. His flying machine was made of wood with two mechanical wings powered by winches and pulleys.

stars, rather than to speculate about them or mathematically analyse them. He confirmed earlier theories about the sun being at the centre of the solar system by thinkers such as Nicholas Copernicus (1473–1543), and proved the mathematical arguments of Johannes Kepler put forward in 1590, but was censured by the church for seeming to contradict the scriptures. He replied that the Bible taught spiritual truth, the world physical truth. More accurately, he had criticized Aristotle and Aquinas. In their systems, the planets were perfect spheres that moved around the earth, making heavenly music as they went. Through the views of a telescope, Galileo had shown that this could not be true; the planets were imperfect. In 1610, he had studied the phases of the moon, and he observed the four large moons of Jupiter. He also discovered sunspots. What the eye could see was different from what Holy Mother Church had taught. After initial interest in his ideas and permission to publish a book that could deal with the Copernican idea as a theory, he was placed under house arrest in 1633, and he agreed not to seek any more publicity for his views.

> *The Bible teaches us how to go to heaven, not how the heavens go.*
>
> GALILEO GALILEI,
> *THE TWO GREAT SYSTEMS OF THE WORLD*

Frontispiece for the 1683 edition of *A Discourse Concerning a New World & Another Planet* by John Wilkins, showing Copernicus, Galileo and Kepler.

René Descartes

The French philosopher René Descartes developed the deduction and observation techniques of Bacon and Galileo further, mapping out the foundation of the modern scientific method.

Descartes (1596–1650) was skilled in mathematics and the use of lenses. In the field of science, he made a lasting contribution with his revision of algebra, and he solved the mystery of the anaclastic. The anaclastic describes when parallel rays of light pass through a fluid and intersect. This was, he demonstrated, because of the variation in the angles of refracted light. Some of his other views did not stand the test of time. For example, he speculated that objects attracted each other through swirling whirlpools of minute particles that interacted with each other. This was abandoned later, after Isaac Newton (1642–1727) suggested the force of gravity.

> *I think, therefore I am.*
>
> RENÉ DESCARTES,
> *MEDITATIONS*

By his observations, Descartes sought to form an initial premise and to test this by further observation. He was rejecting the authority of tradition and seeking to view the world through fresh eyes. For this reason, he is sometimes called 'the first modern philosopher'. His lasting contribution is in the field of epistemology, the science of knowledge.

Cause and effect

Descartes overthrew the Scholastics and their notion of final causes. This stated that each thing was given a purpose in the world. Thus, fire rises and knives cut. They do because that is their direction,

René Descartes with Christina of Sweden, by Louis Michel Dumesnil (1680–1746).

Left: Descartes' universe, showing how matter that filled it was collected in vortices with a star at the centre of each, often orbiting planets. From *Epistolae* by René Descartes, 1668.

their givenness. Descartes looked at prior causes instead, establishing clear processes of cause and effect. He made the world sound less animistic and magical, and more routine and mechanical.

Reductionism

Descartes adopted a reductionist technique. This meant that he broke down physical objects and forces into their component parts and analysed them. They were explicable solely in these terms. He did not reject the existence of an immortal soul, though, or of a creator God. These were spiritual things that could not be so reduced and investigated. He spoke of 'extended substances' and 'thinking substances'. The former were material things, with features such as length, breadth and height. They could be divided again and again into simpler and simpler components. Only thought – spiritual, mental existence – could not be divided. This was the domain of what he called 'clear and distinct ideas'.

THE VISIONARY PHILOSOPHER

Descartes was a soldier for a number of years, and he turned to philosophy as a result of a series of vivid dreams: he was almost thrown over by a whirlwind; he ran into a college for shelter and was given a melon from a distant land by an old friend; and he sat in bed, looking at an encyclopedia and a book of poetry. He read deep meanings into these dreams. He was to explore concepts that resulted in a paradigm shift, shaking his world upside down (the whirlwind), and he found security in the reality of his thinking self and his faith in a good God (the old friend and the gift of a refreshing fruit). He was to commit himself to study and not to military adventure (the books by his bed).

Clear and Distinct Ideas

Descartes spoke of clear and distinct ideas as inner concepts in the mind that could be deduced by the intellect alone, but could be confirmed by observation and sense experience. The greatest of these was the *cogito*, or the thinking self.

When we perceived a basic, singular concept that could not be broken down any further, we had arrived at a 'clear and distinct idea'. This could be a number or an equation, or a concept such as a triangle, or a thing such as liquid. Wax, for example, could exist in a number of states, and might present itself to the senses as hot and liquid, as soft and warm, or as cold and hard. Its underlying properties were the constants in the concept of 'wax'. Concepts such as the self and God were also 'clear and distinct ideas'.

The *cogito* and *Meditations*

Descartes presented his central philosophy in *Meditations on First Principles*. These were six meditations, each of which lasted a day. It was an unusual style to write in, based upon the devotional, spiritual exercises of the time. Descartes wanted to find sure and certain knowledge; information coming through the senses could be misleading, even if it were normally reliable. We might hallucinate, for example.

Could a finite human mind, one tiny speck in the vast universe, conceive of an infinite being unaided?

I should not, however, have the idea of an infinite substance, seeing I am a finite being, unless it were given me by some substance in reality infinite.

RENÉ DESCARTES,
MEDITATIONS

Descartes practised a radical scepticism, doubting everything. The one sure thing he finds is the *cogito*. This is the thinking self, the 'I' in my head. He ends up with one certainty: '*Cogito, ergo sum*' ('I think, therefore I am'). He allies this with belief in a good God who would not place him in a created order that would deceive; the principles of mathematics are also a very reliable guide, and sense observation is also reliable, in general.

Cartesian circles and dualism

Descartes revisits Anselm's ontological argument. For him, God must exist, as the idea of such an infinite reality was planted in his finite mind. It is not something he could have conceived of if it were not real. This is known as the Cartesian circle (from the Latin for Descartes, Cartesius), as it is a form of circular argument.

Cartesian dualism is the idea that mind and body are radically separate, and that mind is the most real and abiding substance. This view has been blamed for a host of problems, such as damage to the environment and even anorexia — a debasement of the body in favour of the intellect. Descartes was much more subtle, however, claiming that mind and body, though two completely separate things, were joined together in a sublime union in a living, breathing human being. A human was a mind/body unity.

SPINOZA

Baruch Spinoza (1632–77) was a Dutch Jew who was excommunicated from the synagogue for his radical views. He challenged Descartes' view that soul and body were two distinct substances. He puzzled over how an immaterial force could cause motion in a physical one, and taught monism. The basic substance of the cosmos was God himself, and there were various modes or levels of being within this. Soul and body represented God's thought and extension, the inward and the outward.

John Locke and Empiricism

John Locke is regarded as the founding father of empiricism, whereby we learn about the world from sense experience alone, and not from some innate ability to see 'clear and distinct ideas' by reason alone.

John Locke (1632–1704) was the son of a lawyer who fought with the Parliamentary forces in the English Civil War. Locke's work *An Essay Concerning Understanding* was published in 1690, although he had been working on it since 1671. It was to exert a widespread influence upon philosophy and science, and it was obligatory reading for the intelligentsia of the 18th century. Descartes had questioned the fixed world view of the Scholastics, and he had thrown open the question of the limits of human knowledge. Locke sought to secularize the medieval sense of limit, recognizing that there would be boundaries to human reason and understanding. We had to work with a little humility in the face of the awesome universe.

The tabula rasa

His central thesis was that we learn through the impact of the external world upon our senses, and our inner, mental faculties

process this data. The act of reflection uses information about things that are really out there. We might imagine and dream all sorts of fabulous things, but they have no reality

Portrait of John Locke by Herman Verelst, 1689.

outside our minds. He rejected Plato's idea of *anamnesis* – that we are born with some innate knowledge of the world from a past life. He also rejected the Cartesian idea that true knowledge began within the mind, with its ability to 'see' clear ideas and concepts such as the triangle or light. We know nothing of triangles unless we

John Locke was witty and charming, cultivating many friendships. He qualified as a doctor of medicine from Oxford, and served the Earl of Shaftesbury as his physician. He had to flee England for Holland when Shaftesbury fell out of favour with the king. There, he developed his ideas and advised William of Orange, being one of the conspirators who organized his succession to the English throne in 1688, ousting the Roman Catholic James II.

see one demonstrated before our eyes, and of light unless we see it blazing at us in candle flame, sunlight or the stars. The concept comes after the experience; ideas are a posteriori and not a priori. He went on to argue that the newborn infant's mind is like a blank slate, a tabula rasa. We are then what life makes us. Surroundings, opportunities and training develop our intellect. These ideas affected views of natural science, giving weight to the skills of observation and experimentation. They also fuelled radical ideas about education and society, for all were born equal, intrinsically.

Though therefore there be several general propositions that meet with constant and ready assent as soon as proposed to men grown up, who have attained the use of more general and abstract ideas, and names standing for them; yet they not being found in those of tender years, who nevertheless know other things, they cannot pretend to universal assent of intelligent persons, and so by no means can be supposed to be innate.

JOHN LOCKE,
*AN ESSAY CONCERNING
HUMAN UNDERSTANDING*

William of Orange, who helped John Locke succeed to the throne in 1688, surveys the field in the heat of battle. *The Battle of the Boyne* by Van Wyke.

Faith and Reason

Locke was pious and found room for God within his system. In his view, however, religious teachings must never be against reason, and all claims to revelation must be judged by this standard.

Locke was concerned to end, wherever possible, the distinction and enmity between faith and reason. Faith, properly understood, concerned things beyond human knowledge. Locke does admit and allow that there are things we cannot fathom with our natural minds, and that a good God might impart extrasensory knowledge of such things, such as the resurrection or the existence of angels, and these are matters of faith alone. They cannot be imposed or forced upon anyone – they are beliefs.

Any special revelations that do not concern simple concepts already understood are liable to be incommunicable, as with the apostle Paul's visit to heaven in a vision. He heard speech that no human could comprehend, and, not surprisingly, could not pass this on.

Beware the enthusiasts!
Locke believed that God had placed in people a natural faculty to understand enough about his design and purpose for the world, with a sense of innate moral law, which is also underscored in the teachings of scripture. God might prompt or inspire our minds by the Holy Spirit to behave in a certain manner, but these are no more than ways of emphasizing the general rules of morality that we discern through reason and in the scriptures as an abiding code. Any personal 'revelations' are to be tested by these things.

Locke, like other rationalists, feared what was then called enthusiasm, an emotive appeal to revelation from God that might be no more than a projection of our fantasies, fears and madness.

If you do not understand the operations of your own finite mind, that thinking thing within you, do not deem it strange that you cannot comprehend the operations of that eternal infinite Mind who made and governs all things, and whom the heaven of heavens cannot contain.

JOHN LOCKE,
AN ESSAY CONCERNING HUMAN UNDERSTANDING

Scholars began to question and challenge the authority of scripture and the basics of Christianity, such as the miracles of Jesus. *Christ Resurrects the Son of the Widow of Nain* by Eustache Le Sueur (1616–55).

God reveals himself through nature and the senses.

Biblical criticism

Locke's calm and rational faith in a deity who was discernible from design and the inner moral conscience opened up a wealth of debate about the authority of the church and of the scriptures – such things were now to be judged by reason. People wanted liberty to think and to act, and there were two unforeseen consequences of Locke's thought. Firstly, many began to turn towards ethics as a social and personal substitute for organized religion. Locke had argued that the moral code in the Bible was none other than that which could be deduced by our own reason.

Secondly, the minor place Locke gave to revelation showed how unimportant it was to him. Later thinkers downplayed this even more, seeing it as no more than the highlighting of what we could find out anyway, with time. The scriptures were studied in a new, critical manner, and many fundamentals of the Christian faith were challenged, such as miracles and the resurrection of Christ. Locke had opened the doors to more than he realized or intended.

Newton's Science

Sir Isaac Newton was another founding father of the modern world. His advances in scientific theory have had abiding influence.

Newton (1642–1727) was born in Lincolnshire, England, the only son of a local yeoman, in the year that Galileo died. His studies introduced him to the new scientific methods, and he read the works of Descartes. This was also at a time when theories of atomism had been revived, which sought a fully materialistic understanding of the structure of the cosmos. Newton's own scientific achievements were outstanding. He was accepted as one of eight associates of the French Acadèmie des Sciences in 1699, and became the President of the Royal Society in 1703. Queen Anne knighted him in 1705, the first scientist to be so honoured. His major works were *Principia Mathematica* and *Opticks*. In the former, he turned his attention to motion and the planets, reconciling ideas of Galileo with the mathematics of Kepler. He suggested the theory of gravity, and postulated that space was infinite. *Opticks*

> *I seem to have been only a boy playing on the sea-shore, and diverting myself in now and then finding a smoother pebble or a prettier shell than ordinary, whilst the great ocean of truth lay all undiscovered before me.*
>
> ISAAC NEWTON

discussed the nature of light and reflection.

Mechanics and mysteries

Newton's universe is often described as mechanical, being an ordered, self-regulating system. God was the First Cause, but set laws within the universe that allowed it to run by itself, rather like a watchmaker with a watch. Newton tended in this direction, but he did not insist that the whole created universe was explicable in this way. For him, gravity was a mysterious force that could not be fully explained or analysed. He also recognized that the universe was subject

Newton ruled the Royal Observatory in an autocratic manner. He earned the mistrust of the astronomer royal, John Flamsteed, by using many of his researches for his *Principia Mathematica*, but not acknowledging him in later editions. In 1701, he became warden of the Mint, moving from Cambridge to London. His scientific studies finished there, and he ended his life comfortably on a salary of about 2,000 pounds per annum.

Illustration of a Newtonian experiment showing that the coloured spectrum resulting from white light passing through a glass prism cannot be split any further. From *Mathematical Elements of Natural Philosophy Confirm'd by Experiment* (1747) by J.T. Desgauliers – a popular explanation of Newton's *Principia Mathematica*.

to entropy, the gradual running down of energy. It was not a perpetual motion machine.

His belief in God as the necessary First Cause led him to explore mystical ideas, such as alchemy, and esoteric writings known as the *Hermetica*. He published works on the scriptures, seeking to understand the prophecies in the book of Daniel and the Gospel of John. Other views of his were unorthodox, and he sent a manuscript to John Locke in 1690, arguing that the Trinity was a later addition to the New Testament. He never published this, fearing that public

opinion would turn against him for the worst.

Summing up

Newton became the ideal scientist, and set the paradigm for later thinkers and researchers. The 17th century closed on an emerging new world of science and reason. Bacon, Galileo, Descartes, Locke and Newton were to leave a legacy that blossomed in the 18th century as the Enlightenment.

THE ENLIGHTENMENT

The 18th century was the age of the Enlightenment. This eventually centred in Paris, but had roots in England and spread across Europe and out to the American colonies. Seventeenth-century developments in science and observation had laid the foundation. France and England were leading world powers and exerted tremendous influence.

England had undergone the Glorious Revolution in 1688–89, when William of Orange and Mary, daughter of Charles I, ascended the throne. This established a constitutional monarchy and gave Parliament the Bill of Rights, protecting its powers. The Toleration Act followed in 1689, allowing religious dissenters freedom of

The Establishment of the Academy of Sciences by Louis XIV in 1666 and the Foundation of the Observatory (1667). Painting by Henri Testelin (1616–75).

worship. As a result, some say the Enlightenment began in 1688.

The church began to lose its influence as an institution – traditional doctrines and scriptures were questioned in the new Age of Reason. Galileo and Descartes had had to be careful of the power of the popes and the Inquisition, but a shift could be discerned as early as 1648, when the Thirty Years' War ended with the Peace of Westphalia. This sought to promote peace and toleration between rival versions of Christianity in Europe, and the pope was ignored when he declared its clauses to be null and void.

The old order was being shaken off, and the modern age had begun. Various thinkers and movements began to map out the implications of this for education, government, religion, science and philosophy. There were vested power interests, though, in the nobility and the crown, as well as in the bishops. They did not always go quietly. The 18th century was an age of revolution.

Contents

There is a mighty light which spreads itself over the world, especially in those two free nations of England and Holland...

LORD SHAFTESBURY'S LETTER
TO JEAN LE CLERC, 1706

115

The Philosophes

Paris was the intellectual centre of Europe in the 18th century, with its philosophes and the ambitious project to compile the volumes of the *Encyclopédie* to disseminate and connect up many fields of knowledge.

The philosophes were the Parisian intelligentsia who formed the radical wing of the Enlightenment, discussing ideas in journals, books, coffee houses and the salons. Foreign visitors were welcome; David Hume (1711–76), from Edinburgh, and Samuel Johnson (1709–84), from England, as well as the American Benjamin Franklin (1706–90) all attended salons. The salons were open houses owned by women. They acted as hostesses and entertained the philosophes. These 'enlightened mistresses' joined in debates, read widely and corresponded with the philosophes. Women in general found a greater role in intellectual life. Voltaire's companion Emilie du Châtelet wrote a major commentary on Newton, for example.

Voltaire (1694–1778) urged the philosophes to unite into a 'Party of Reason', but it was Denis Diderot (1713–84) who brought their ideas together in the *Encyclopédie*. This was originally to be a translation of Ephraim Chambers' *Cyclopaedia*, published in Edinburgh in 1727.

Diderot worked with the mathematician D'Alembert (1717–83). It took over 20 years to produce the first edition, the first volume of which appeared in 1751. The 17-volume set was composed of about 72,000 entries or articles, written by a vast group of philosophes, including Voltaire and Rousseau, and accompanied by another 11 volumes of plates. This was a bold attempt to integrate knowledge and show the connectedness of learning; Diderot translated '*encyclopédie*', following the Greek language, as 'the interrelation

Coffee houses in England and the Continent were places where ideas were exchanged and discussed. They were meeting places for the literati and the intelligentsia. There were 400 in Westminster alone by the middle of the 18th century. Traders would meet, share ideas and conduct their business in these establishments. Lloyd's of London was formed in 1691 from Lloyd's coffee house.

In truth, the aim of an encyclopedia is to collect all the knowledge scattered over the face of the earth, to present its general outlines and structures to the men with whom we live and to transmit this to those who will come after us, so that the work of past centuries may be useful to the following centuries.

DENIS DIDEROT,
ENCYCLOPÉDIE

of all knowledge'. He used Bacon's analogy of the tree, with its branches of memory, reason and imagination. Attention was given to the *métiers*, the arts and the crafts. There was little time for anything not open to study by

Illustrations of pin-making from Denis Diderot's *Encyclopédie*.

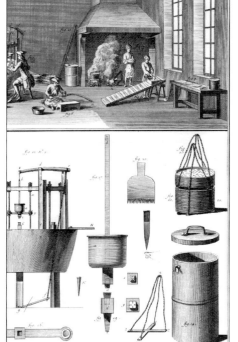

reason, though; the doctrines of the church were a minor entry.

The *Encyclopédie* was read widely, and it was reported that royalty consulted it in discussions and parlour games at dinner parties. The group had

One who, trampling on prejudice, tradition, universal consent, authority — in a word, all that enslaves most minds — dares to think for himself... to admit nothing except on the testimony of his experience and his reason.

ENCYCLOPÉDIE,
ON 'PHILOSOPHES'

their enemies, and reactionaries attacked them as plagiarists, hypocrites, heretics and plotters. The entire project was always in danger of being halted and had constant problems with censorship.

The 'self' as fiction?

If our ideas and perceptions are formed by external impulses, then what are we? A new form of materialism and atheism was propagated by thinkers who followed Locke. Voltaire wrote of a dream in which it is proposed that we are nothing but the sum of many tendencies. The Scottish philosopher David Hume despaired that the self was a fiction, a string of moments, ever moving on. He lived in France from 1734 to 1737, imbibing the views of the philosophes.

The Consent of the People

The Enlightenment questioned the old social order, with its hereditary privileges and traditions, seeking to base government upon reason, and laws upon the consent of the people.

John Locke wrote against the background of the English Civil War (1642–48), a revolution that had overthrown an autocratic monarch and experimented with constitutional monarchy. In his *Two Treatises of Government* (1690), he argued that the consent of the people is the sole basis of authority for any form of government. The monarch is not to use his or her

REVOLUTIONS

The American War of Independence was forced upon reluctant colonials who had petitioned the English government for years. The opening words of the Declaration of Independence paraphrase Locke's words of years earlier.

America was indeed a land of opportunity, where the divisions between rich and poor were not as pronounced as in Europe, but the institution of slavery spoiled this dream. Thomas Jefferson, one of the authors of the Declaration of Independence, was a slave owner and this troubled his conscience. What rights were the slaves given?

The French Revolution began as the commoners formed their own national

assembly, frustrated with the intransigence of the absolutist Louis XVI. The crowds stormed the Bastille on 14 July 1789, and a new constitution was declared, the Declaration of the Rights of Man and Citizen. The revolution's slogan was pure Enlightenment – 'liberty, equality, fraternity'. This all went terribly wrong, though, when France was threatened by invasion and the unruly mob made demands that could not be met. Liberty gave way to terror under Robespierre (1758–94), when, during three months in 1794, over 1,400 people were killed by the guillotine.

The Signing of the Declaration of Independence by John Trumbull (1756–1843).

Left: Engraving from 1804 of the storming of the Bastille by Parisians led by the Grenadier Guards on 14 July 1776.

We hold these truths to be self-evident, that all Men are created equal, that they are endowed by their creator with certain unalienable Rights, that among these are Life, Liberty, and the Pursuit of Happiness.

THE DECLARATION OF INDEPENDENCE

power in an arbitrary manner. If the monarch abuses power, then the people 'are at liberty to provide for themselves'. In other words, rebellion is sometimes justified. Government is to safeguard the preservation of 'life, liberty and property'.

Voltaire

The French philosopher Voltaire was born a commoner, and his satirical writings often brought him into disrepute – he spent a year in the Bastille in 1717. After challenging an aristocrat to a duel, he fled to England in 1726 for two and a half years. He wrote a series of letters from there, which purported to comment upon English customs and traditions. In fact, they were indirect critiques of French society by comparison and implication. He comments upon religious toleration in England, and stresses how free enterprise allowed real opportunities and led to England being a great nation. Parliament was praised for having deposed a king, and any future monarchs have their 'hands tied for doing evil'. Taxes were paid by all, noble or commoner, unlike in France, where the nobility and higher clergy were exempt. There was equality before the law.

Voltaire seemed fascinated by the mildly eccentric Quakers he encountered in England, and he admired them for their refusal to be dominated by any clergy.

The Human Machine

Enlightenment views of human nature stressed the physical, the material and the mechanical. Searching questions were asked about experience and perception, and the nature of reality.

Newton's ideas led many thinkers to frame the world and human beings in mathematical, mechanical terms. Some sought to define the world purely in terms of matter and motion, and they applied this to human psychology too. If human consciousness was no more than a series of sensations from the external world, then the idea of a soul was seen as unnecessary. Offroy de la Mettrie published *L'Homme Machine (Man the Machine)* in 1748, seeking to explain all human faculties in materialist terms. Claude-Adrien Helvétius published *De l'Esprit (On Mind)* in 1758, which argued that all thought and will is a consequence of sense impression received.

What is real?

Locke had returned to the medieval idea that there were definite limits to human understanding, but he had secularized it. He insisted that we were limited in our knowledge because we relied on our senses. Only what was mediated through them was known to us.

The trouble is that we cannot get outside our own heads and sense perceptions. We have a cluster of images and ideas, but we cannot know external reality in itself. He

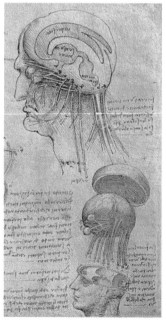

We cannot move beyond the confines of our own heads. Pen-and-ink study of the anatomy of the human brain.

Where am I, or what? From what causes do I derive my existence, and to what condition shall I return?

DAVID HUME,
A TREATISE OF HUMAN NATURE

Engraving of David Hume by Allan Ramsay.

differentiated between primary and secondary qualities. Primary qualities belong to the measurable aspects of external reality such as shape; secondary qualities were more subjective and belonged within our perceptions, such as colour and taste.

Hume was an empiricist, but he struggled with the limitations and absurdities of this philosophy. He saw that facts formed by observation were always provisional; one could always see something different one day that would make you revise your theory; for example, you might assume all swans were white until one day you saw a black one. He also realized that our rational and scientific concepts are themselves in our minds; they are our constructions and might not correspond to reality. Thus, 'causality' is a concept in our minds. We can watch a ball being struck and the motion that results, but causality itself is still an abstraction.

Being human is like being trapped in a sealed movie theatre with our interpretations alone on the screen telling us what is 'out there'.

KANT'S SPECTACLES

The German philosopher Immanuel Kant (1724–1804) sought a way out of the frustrating cul-de-sac of seeing knowledge as arising within the mind, or from outside stimulation. He argued that there are two aspects to reality, the world of the phenomena (the world of appearances that we perceive) and that of the noumena (the inner reality of things known only to God). All reality is filtered through the lenses of our experience and interpretation. Kant argued that far from being a passive recipient of external stimuli, the mind has innate faculties to perceive, conceptualize and create. We create our own mental picture of the world, and thus make sense of serial, sensory data. We do not learn from observation alone, and our ideas are not the product of cumulative experiences, but of a priori intuitions as well. Kant was straddling the views of both rationalists and empiricists, showing how both were inadequate. There is that within us that is somehow attuned, from birth, to perceive the world around us.

Reactions to Reason

Poets, artists and philosophers reacted to the excessive use of reason as well as religious views, suggesting an alternative vision of the world.

William Blake (1757–1827) was an eccentric, visionary poet and artist who embraced a romantic belief in imagination rather than reason. He saw angels in a tree when he was a boy, and the face of God in the rising sun. He wrote about England as 'Albion', a spiritual place that needed to be free of the shackles of rationalism and the Industrial Revolution. He railed against 'the dark, satanic mills' and the mechanization of life, speaking of 'cruel Works / Of many Wheels I view, wheel without wheel, with cogs tyrannic'.

Blake was a man of the Enlightenment in other ways, though, admiring the early days of the French Revolution and despising totalitarian regimes. In his poem 'Garden of Love', he complains that 'Priests in black gowns, were walking their rounds, / And binding with briars, my joys and desires.'

NIETZSCHE

Friedrich Nietzsche (1844–1900) was a German philosopher who railed against the Enlightenment and the false confidence he saw in working out what was true and what was ethical. He used the disciplines of historical enquiry against philosophy, showing the genealogy of an idea or moral position. He attacked Christianity, seeing this as a faith for the weak, rather than a way of compassion that sought to include all. His questioning of 'truth' laid the foundations of later, postmodern thought.

Rousseau – 'back to nature'

Jean-Jacques Rousseau (1712–78) was Swiss-born and a philosophe in Paris working on the *Encyclopédie*. His ideas began to diverge from the other philosophes. He taught that society and culture became progressively more degenerate and inhumane the more

> *Man's perceptions are not bound by organs of perception; he perceives more than sense (though ever so acute) can discover.*
>
> WILLIAM BLAKE,
> *THERE IS NO NATURAL RELIGION*

Man was born free and he is everywhere in chains.

JEAN-JACQUES ROUSSEAU,
THE SOCIAL CONTRACT

vain and empty titles with all their pomp came into being. Living in an age of travel and newly discovered lands (this was the age of Captain Cook, for example), he spoke of the 'noble savage' who was closer to nature and fairer than his/her modern counterparts. He despised sophistication and grew tired of the salons with their music, card games and parades of learning by fellow philosophes – it was all empty and superficial. Real enlightenment took the thinker into oneself in self-aware reflection. His own conscience, rather than any other person, or moral 'authority', was to be his guide. He sought solace in the countryside, alone for hours reflecting upon the wonder of the Supreme Being, when 'a sweet and profound reverie takes hold of the senses so that you lose yourself, with a delicious intoxication…' His 'back to nature' ideals inspired the later Romantic movement.

Allegorical painting with a portrait of Rousseau, along with the tricolore and other symbols of the French Revolution. *Revolutionary Allegory in Honour of Rousseau* by H. Jeaurat de Bertry (1728–96).

'advanced' they became. He argued that the lust for private property was the root of inequality, and that primitive tribes had shared resources and respected the land. Powerful individuals had enslaved others and stolen land. When money was invented as a sign of wealth rather than actual goods, more unreality entered society, and

Faith and the Enlightenment

The Enlightenment was an age of great faith and spiritual movements, despite the materialist emphasis. Many of the philosophes held to a belief in a Supreme Being.

The philosophes, like Locke and Newton before them, believed, on the whole, in God as creator. In a mechanical universe, a First Cause was required to give it being and order. The natural laws that governed it were seen as being placed there by God to ensure its order and harmony. This was the idea of the divine watchmaker, as in William Paley's analogy of 1802. He argued that if you found a watch on the road, you would look at its intricacy and deduce that it must have a designer; so, too, must the world.

Even the more materialistic and atheistic thinkers saw that religion was necessary to guide the masses and to instil moral order. Voltaire famously quipped that if God did not exist, then we would have to invent him!

Scepticism

God might exist, but we could say hardly anything about him apart from what was rational. Hume pointed out that much of the Gospels could not be believed. Miracles were seen as being impossible in a rational universe. If God created natural laws, then he would not seek to tinker with them and suspend them. This was to usher in a wave of critical studies of the life of Christ that sought to strip away the supernatural. The ideas of the various 'Lives' can be summed up by the Liberal Protestantism of Adolf von Harnack's beliefs in *History of Dogma* (1886–90). He defined Christ's teaching as being about 'the Fatherhood of God and the brotherhood of man'. A First Cause and the moral law were all that the Enlightenment would allow.

Revivalists

Others reacted against the arid rationalism and scepticism of the age by embracing a more passionate, experiential faith, what a rationalist would call 'enthusiasm'. This had stirred in the 17th century as a reaction against the emerging rationalism of thinkers such as Descartes and the overly intellectual faith of the

D.F. Strauss's *Life of Jesus Critically Examined* (1835) proposed that Jesus' miracles were coded symbols of ethical and spiritual insights. This was an immense work, covering 15,000 words in two volumes. It ushered in a more thorough study of the life of Jesus.

Chromolithograph published in 1888 showing John Wesley, the founder of Methodism, preaching.

Scholastics. The Jansenists and the Quietists influenced the Roman Catholic Church. These stressed that a personal experience of divine grace was necessary to live a Christian life. The French mathematician and philosopher Blaise Pascal (1623–62) was influenced by the Jansenists and underwent a profound conversion experience.

From about half past ten in the evening until about half past midnight.
Fire.
God of Abraham, God of Isaac, God of Jacob, not of the philosophers and scholars. Certainty, certainty, heartfelt, joy, peace.
God of Jesus Christ…
The world forgotten, and everything except God…
Joy, joy, joy, tears of joy.

BLAISE PASCAL, 'MEMORIAL'

John Wesley (1703–91) had been a highly religious young man at Oxford with a group of pious friends. Their strict, methodical discipline gained them the nickname 'Methodists'. Wesley had a personal conversion experience at a meeting in Aldersgate Street in London, when he said that he felt his heart was strangely warmed and he believed in Christ alone for salvation. Wesley travelled around England and beyond, managing an average of 8,000 miles a year on horseback. He drew huge crowds who often fell to the ground under conviction of sin. These movements reminded people that religion involved the heart and not just the head.

Leaps of Faith and Emerging Spirit

There were original and imaginative contributions to religious thought and theology in the late 18th and early 19th centuries, which sought to use Enlightenment ideas but to move beyond them. Søren Kierkegaard and Georg Wilhelm Friedrich Hegel are two outstanding thinkers of this period.

The German philosopher Hegel (1770–1831) worked towards a theory of everything. He argued that the universe should be open to reason, and one day could be understood in its totality. Human beings, possessed of a rational mind, were in a position to aspire to this goal. He used terms such as 'Spirit', 'Reason', 'Mind' and the 'Absolute' to refer to totality, existence and God. God was an imminent force at work in the cosmos, gradually unveiling itself in the minds of humans. Christ was a foretaste of this, the incarnation being a reference to the incarnating of Spirit in each rational soul. D.F. Strauss was influenced by Hegel's obscure and weighty tome, *Phenomenology of Spirit*, incorporating many Hegelian ideas in his work.

In the long climb to the Absolute, Hegel understood that there was a process of realizing new ideas. He saw that a thesis

Only one man ever understood me... And he didn't understand me.
GEORG HEGEL, ON HIS DEATHBED

Engraving of Georg Hegel by Lazarus Gottlieb Sichling (1812–63).

and an antithesis were often only partial insights into truth, and that a synthesis of the two poles brought about greater understanding and harmony. This developmental philosophy influenced 19th-century thinkers, particularly Karl Marx.

Kierkegaard and existence

Søren Kierkegaard (1813–55) was born in Copenhagen and

later attended the university there. He was left an inheritance by his father, and could pursue a life as an independent writer. He turned his attention to philosophy, theology and literary studies. He was a lonely, troubled individual who had been brought up in the Lutheran church. He felt that

Watercolour portrait of Søren Kierkegaard by Christian Klaestrup (1820–82).

The secret in life is that everyone must sew it for himself…

SØREN KIERKEGAARD,
FEAR AND TREMBLING

Kierkegaard fell from a tree as a child and suffered a curvature of the spine. He grew up with a sharp wit and cultivated an eccentric image, as he was a social outsider. His father had educated him in this way for precociousness, and one of Kierkegaard's writings has a story of such a father and son, who are both in 'silent despair'.

actions and paths in life. His writings push us back upon ourselves, reminding the reader of this freedom. He criticized Hegel for trying to prescribe the future: 'It may be that life can only be understood backwards, but it has to be lived forwards.'

He was a passionate believer in Christ, but not Christendom or the established church. He spoke of 'smuggling Christ into Christendom', and rejected any attempts at providing objective proofs of the Gospel. The Gospel was to be lived, not argued. Faith had to be a leap in the dark of paradox and doubt, a personal, free choice of commitment.

he was always destined to be an outsider.

He reacted against the stress on reason, the abstractions of theology and the moral rules of his day. Ideas and reality had been cut adrift from each other, and not enough emphasis was placed upon our actual experience and the actual, radical freedom that we each exercise to choose different

Summing up

The Enlightenment freed reason to work its wonders and brought new technology. It brought freedom from tyranny and the concept of human rights. However, it also brought exploitation, pollution and revolution. The expressive and the imaginative are also part of human life.

MODERNISM AND POSTMODERNISM

The modern age, the age of Enlightenment, was one of reason, the rise of science and new inventions. Invention and technology gathered speed from the middle of the 19th century to the early years of the 20th century. The rapid spread of technology in the 20th century birthed a period known as 'modernity' and a movement known as 'modernism'. Modernity was characterized by speed, by faster means of travel and communication. Trains, cars, aeroplanes, cinema and radio brought a new way of seeing and feeling

The Wright brothers' biplane. From a set of cards published c. 1915.

L'Aéroplane de Kress.

VÉRITABLE EXTRAIT DE VIANDE LIEBIG.

about the world, and popular music reflected this high energy. It was a period of hope and a belief in progress – somehow, life could only get better.

Modernism emerged as a philosophical and artistic movement that probed deeper into the underlying rhythms of modernity. This movement was wedded to the new technology, driven by invention, possibility and the power of reason, but aware of the contradictions too. What of the emotions, the poetic and the irrational? What values could still be held, and what terror could be inflicted with the new science? Modernity produced the 'unsinkable' ship, the *Titanic*, and revolutionized the battlefield in the First World War as machine guns faced lines of disciplined cavalry.

The Second World War brought modernity to a close, with its weapons of mass destruction and the cold science of the Holocaust. The avant-garde swept through the arts, breaking up traditional formulas and patterns, rearranging and suggesting. It was a time of uncertainty and disorientation, as well as excitement.

Contents

History is more or less bunk.
It's tradition. We don't want tradition.
We want to live in the present, and the
only history that is worth a tinker's damn
is the history we make today.
HENRY FORD,
CHICAGO TRIBUNE, 25 MAY 1916

lane des frères Wright,

Literature, Language and Philosophy

Writers broke established literary conventions with experimental works, linguists sought to understand the structure of language and its arbitrary meanings, and philosophers struggled with what language could say and with human existence.

T.S. Eliot's *The Waste Land* and James Joyce's *Ulysses* were both published in 1922. Both writers had been experimenting with poetry and novel forms before this, but these two works caught the spirit of the age. They were Modernist texts par excellence. They are hard to read, and weave various literary and historical references together. *Ulysses* uses conventional narrative, stream of consciousness, letters, and narratives that could come from a drama script. These works dig into the irrational and are fascinated with a sense of the primitive. Echoes of ancient myths and practices underlie them, and Eliot was indebted to Sir James Frazer's work, *The Golden Bough*.

Primitivism influenced artists such as the Surrealists, but also the Fauves ('wild beasts'), such as Henri Matisse (1869–1954). They collected ethnic artefacts and incorporated African images into their art, as did Pablo Picasso in *Les Demoiselles d'Avignon* (1907), with a hint of African masks. The notion of the primitive also figured in psychoanalysis and the writings of Sigmund Freud.

Statue of James Joyce by Marjorie Fitzgibbon, Dublin, Republic of Ireland.

Philosophy

Early 20th-century philosophy tended to be dominated by logical analysis. The Vienna Circle, or the logical positivists, argued that philosophy was really a subdivision of empirical science. It was a useful tool to analyse concepts and to clarify. All talk

D.H. Lawrence (1885–1930) wrote about releasing passions that had been repressed by social taboo and convention, seeing the primitive as a more authentic, honest existence.

of metaphysics was stuff and nonsense. A thing only had meaning if it was empirically testable. This movement

Writer and poet T.S. Eliot.

The Romans and Greeks found everything human. Everything had a face, and a human voice. Men spoke, and their fountains piped an answer.

D.H. LAWRENCE,
FANTASIA OF THE UNCONSCIOUS

LANGUAGE

Ferdinand de Saussure (1857–1913) pioneered the study of linguistics with his *Cours de Linguistique Générale* in 1916. He spoke of the relationship between the signifier (the word for something) and the signified (the object spoken of). He pointed out that the relationship between the two was arbitrary and culturally conditioned. Our terms were human constructs. 'Thinking' and 'making' were thus closely connected.

Of what we cannot speak we must remain silent.

LUDWIG WITTGENSTEIN,
TRACTATUS LOGICO-PHILOSOPHICUS

influenced thinkers at Cambridge such as A.J. Ayer (1910–89) and Bertrand Russell (1872–1970). Russell worked with logical atomism, stripping sentences down to their component parts, and arguing that a component represented an impression in the mind caused by an external stimulus. This world was all that there was; as another of the Cambridge thinkers, Ludwig Wittgenstein (1889–1951), said in his early work, 'The world is all that is the case.' Metaphysics is a problem, because philosophers try to say things that cannot be said. This movement back to language is known as 'the linguistic turn', and it influenced modern philosophy greatly. Human language is limited, being representational of physical objects, and it is socially constructed (remember Saussure). What place is left, though, for the emotions and the creative imagination?

Evolution

Charles Darwin revolutionized 19th-century thought with his theory of the evolution of species by the process of natural selection. It challenged established biological, geological and religious views.

Darwin (1809–82) studied medicine at Edinburgh, and then theology at Cambridge. He was fascinated by natural life, and he collected insects and geological specimens. His botany professor succeeded in getting him a place aboard HMS *Beagle* for an exploratory trip to Patagonia (1831–36). He collected many specimens, and observed plants and animals on his travels. He began to establish himself in the scientific community, becoming secretary of the Geological Society (1838–41). His researches were written up in note form by 1844, and published as *On the Origin of Species by Means of Natural Selection* in 1859. He followed this with *The Descent of Man*, which speculated about human evolution from apes. Darwin had noted differences between creatures in the same species, such as tortoises on the Galápagos Islands, or ostriches in Argentina. There were different sizes and forms depending upon the

A cartoon from 1874, showing Darwin as an ape himself.

I have called this principle, by which each slight variation, if useful, is preserved, by the term of Natural Selection.

CHARLES DARWIN,
THE ORIGIN OF SPECIES

environment. He had read Thomas Malthus's *An Essay on the Principle of Population* (1798). Malthus stressed how life was a struggle for existence, between growing populations and over limited food supplies. All of this material crystallized as the theory of natural selection.

Religion

Theologians had taken the opening chapters of Genesis as literal history, arguing for a special creation 'from scratch' of each new species in a period of six days. When a species became extinct and a new one was discovered, it was assumed that a new act of special creation had taken place.

The initial response to Darwin's ideas from the church was hostile. The preacher C.H. Spurgeon declared

Charles Darwin stated that he had a sense of overwhelming awe when studying the make-up of the human eye, and of how this amazing item had developed from simple light-sensitive cells in primitive sea creatures.

evolution a 'monstrous error'. Bishop Wilberforce of Oxford poured witty scorn upon the idea that our ancestors were apes, though he was bested in the debate by the scientist T.H. Huxley. Gradually, theologians found creative ways to integrate evolution and faith: the survival of the fittest needed cooperation and compassion, and the long chain of events that unfolded to show the cosmos in all its splendour must have been by design and not by chance. Genesis was to be read symbolically, with a 'day' meaning 'thousands of years'.

Darwin was not an atheist, but an agnostic, believing in the likelihood of a First Cause who imprinted Laws upon nature.

NATURAL SELECTION

Natural selection teaches the survival of the fittest. Living organisms have to adapt to their surroundings, or they will become extinct. Those that did adapt, slowly, over generations, passed on their favourable genetic mutations through their DNA, and thus their line survived. Thus, moths that develop dusky wings among dark trees are more likely to survive than those with brightly coloured wings. *Homo sapiens* walked upright and had a bigger brain, being able to invent

and to master the environment. Thus, we survived and other hominid races died out. Darwin's theory has been criticized for being cruel and amoral; far-right thinkers have sought to use his ideas to justify sterilization campaigns and the enslaving of races. Darwin taught no such thing. He saw the human ability to cooperate as crucial to our survival skills. It is easier to erect a tent in a storm if people help each other, for example.

Existence

The earlier experiential protest of Kierkegaard came alive in the phenomenology of Edmund Husserl and Martin Heidegger, and in the existentialism of Jean-Paul Sartre.

Husserl (1859–1938) stressed that the only things we can be sure about are found in immediate, raw experience, in other words, what is true and present to our consciousness. This was primary – not debates about innate ideas or what the external world formed in our minds. We cannot say that something exists, only that someone has a series of sensations featuring that object or directed towards it.

He presented his key theories in *Ideas* (1913). He coined the term 'noema' for the thought world that is our conscious experience, with all its features and information. We cannot step outside of ourselves, though, to get at reality itself. He thus rejected any place for God in his system, for metaphysics spoke of things

> *I must accomplish a phenomenological reduction: I must exclude all that is transcendentally posited.*
>
> EDMUND HUSSERL,
> THE IDEA OF PHENOMENOLOGY

> *Time is the meaning of being.*
>
> MARTIN HEIDEGGER,
> BEING AND TIME

Paradox of Time by Arman Fernandez (b. 1936).

beyond ourselves. His motto was 'Truth dwells in the inner man.'

Being

Husserl's pupil Martin Heidegger (1889–1976) spoke of 'Being' rather than theories of the inner essence of things. He was convinced that the Greeks (starting with Plato)

Heidegger taught at Marburg and Freiburg universities in Germany, and was an enthusiastic supporter of Hitler at first, earning him a suspension from teaching from 1945 to 1950.

had 'fallen into metaphysics', locating the most real in the abstract and eternal, rather than in the here and now. He was obscure and mystical at times, especially in his major work *Being and Time* (1927). Human *being* is called *Dasein*, and this 'thisness' is thrown into being rather like clay on a potter's wheel. It 'ek-sists', standing out from nothingness. *Dasein* is temporal, and human life thus has its being in time. Time encloses and defines being. Is it its very and only meaning?

Free to be

Jean-Paul Sartre (1905–80) sought authentic existence in our free choices; life is what we make it, it does not just make us. There is no meaning or purpose that we do not create; 'Everything that exists is born for no reason,' as he said in his novel, *Nausea*.

His was an atheistic but moral vision, and his major work on ideas was *Being and Nothingness* (1943). His 'life is what you make it' philosophy was abused in the 1960s as a selfish creed of hedonistic liberalism, but

Man is condemned to be free.

JEAN-PAUL SARTRE,
*EXISTENTIALISM
IS A HUMANISM*

Sartre had a strong sense of 'being-in-the-world' – the need to relate to others. It was ethical and worthwhile to act on behalf of yourself and others to create greater freedom in society. The 'Other' was a curse as well as a blessing, though, for we each seek to be seen as we would like to be seen. There is an emotional struggle, as we are constantly judged and exposed. In this sense, as one of his characters in the play *In Camera* says, 'Hell is other people.'

Deep being

Existentialism also influenced theology; God was to be found in the flow of life, within existence, and not just 'out there'. Paul Tillich (1886–1965), for example, spoke of the divine as 'the Ground of our Being', and others speak of 'Holy Being'.

Psychoanalysis

The research and theories of Freud revolutionized our understanding of the self. He exposed hidden depths to the psyche that were irrational.

The Austrian Sigmund Freud (1856–1939) experimented with different therapeutic techniques on emotionally disturbed patients. He preferred the free-association technique, whereby he listened to the stories and ramblings of patients, looking for clues and links. His case studies led him

At bottom God is nothing more than an exalted father.

SIGMUND FREUD, *TOTEM AND TABOO*

to develop a new theory of the human mind. Whereas the Enlightenment (and various philosophers going back to Plato) had seen reason as the dominant force in the psyche, Freud saw this as rather ephemeral. The rational ego was the tip of an iceberg. Beneath this was a censor, filtering out painful and difficult experiences and

ANCIENT MYTHS COME ALIVE

Freud sometimes used classical myths to symbolize deep truths about the psyche. The myth of Narcissus tells the story of a young man who falls in love with his own reflection in a pool. He pines away for unrequited love and cannot leave the place.

Freud saw human desire as basically selfish, as the desire to possess the other and to be at the centre of our existence. In our psychological development, we could easily become locked in the narcissistic (self-centred) stage. We needed to learn how to form

relationships with give and take, to be socialized, to live a more balanced life, and to form sexual, loving relationships.

Freud also used the old story of Oedipus, who had killed his own father by mistake and had married his mother. He spoke of the Oedipus complex in our development. We assert ourselves or detach ourselves from parental authority, but the will of the father is internalized as the voice of the conscience. He speculated that religion had its roots in this internalization, whereby God is an illusion, a projection of the internalized father.

heart', with all its mysteries and passions.

Freud's free-association method included the retelling of memorable dreams. They were an important resource. Freud published *The Interpretation of Dreams* in 1900. Dreams could reveal deep feelings in coded form.

Seek balance

Freud saw therapy as providing a balance, a way of handling deep desires and frustrations that often arose from childhood trauma. By opening these up in psychotherapy, and by straightening them out, as it were, a client could then leave neuroses behind and live a more normal, integrated life. Freud saw neurosis as a flight from pain into irrational behaviour or fears.

He applied reason to deeply held beliefs and used logical methods in his analysis, but he succeeded in overthrowing the rational by asserting that the id was the deepest part of our psyches, a vast reservoir of the irrational.

Narcissus by Karl Pawlowitsch Bruellow (1799–1852).

memories, which he called the superego. Then there was the deepest layer of the psyche, the id. This was a vast, unconscious sea of raw feelings, memories and urges. It was akin to what the ancients had called 'the

Marxism

Karl Marx developed a theory of history and politics that was to shake attitudes in the 19th century and shape the first part of the 20th century.

Marx (1818–83), as a young man in his native Germany, was influenced by the Romantic movement that saw humanity as struggling for freedom against various social forces. He also imbibed Hegel's philosophy, and allied himself at first with the Young Hegelians. They adapted and criticized Hegel in significant ways. They rejected his idea that religion was a picturesque form of philosophy. Rather, they saw religion as so much superstition. Only the individual mind and self-consciousness was its own arbiter of truth, and all external authorities, human or divine, were to be swept aside.

They also rejected Hegel's sense of reason or the Absolute as the universal force behind the world: reason dwelt within individuals alone.

Marx went further, and argued that the state was the product of economic forces. If those were changed, then a new form of society could emerge, and a new consciousness. He

Karl Marx, radical economist and a founding father of Communism.

Working Men of All Countries, Unite!

KARL MARX AND FRIEDRICH ENGELS, *COMMUNIST MANIFESTO*

also left the Young Hegelians behind in asserting that emancipation from religion would not bring a fairer world. Economic change was needed. He left Germany for Paris and met Friedrich Engels (1820–95), with whom he collaborated on many works, including the *Communist Manifesto* (1848).

Marx's communist vision saw history as a gradual unfolding of a socialist system. In the early stages, there were hereditary, feudal classes. Those who benefited from the labour of the many without payment were the exploiters, and the mass of labourers were the exploited. The rise of capitalism and industrialization saw a new class system, with the private owners of the means of production as the exploiters.

THE UTOPIAN VISION

Marx believed that capitalism must give way to socialism, and a communist form of society. As more become involved in production, and technology allows cheaper and more plentiful goods, then there will be a shift. People will demand more of a share, and the process will become more democratic and communitarian. There will be a transition to collective ownership. Marx never explained how this would take place, and he did not devote any space to describing how such a society might be organized, beyond the maxim, 'from each according to his ability, to each according to his needs'. There is a degree of Hegelian philosophy in this vision, which has been seen as a secularized form of Judeo-Christian eschatology ('the end times'). The idea of different forms of society struggling over the ages to form a gradual ascent to communism is akin to Hegel's dialectical method of thesis/antithesis and synthesis.

Lenin harangues the deputies of the second Soviet Congress in the Smolny Palace, St Petersberg.

In *Das Kapital* (1867), Marx argues that capitalism is self-replicating, running on internal laws, such as supply and demand and the role of market forces. The weak can be neglected as they are of no perceived value.

Faith and Modernism

The old assurance that progress was inevitable, and that the light of reason would advance as an unstoppable force, was shattered with the outbreak of the First World War.

The First World War (1914–18) shook the optimism that had driven Liberal Protestantism. Three movements, broadly speaking, arose in the wake of modernism: fundamentalism, demythologizing and neo-orthodoxy.

Fundamentalism

In the late 19th and early 20th centuries, various groups of American Protestants gathered to defend their faith against modernism (understood here as a theological movement that questioned the authority of scripture and rejected miracles). A series of 12 tracts, *The Fundamentals*, was issued in 1909, stressing the key points of the faith, such as the divinity of Jesus Christ, the virgin birth, the atonement and the resurrection. Gradually, these groups embraced a view of scripture that taught verbal inerrancy and suspected any symbolic interpretations. Thus, clever and sophisticated attempts to square Genesis with the theory of evolution were rejected; the world was made in six days and that is a fact. This literalism became known as 'fundamentalism'. Ironically, in seeking to combat the fruits of the Enlightenment, these groups had elevated objective facts (very much a rational position) over against the poetic and the expressive. Earlier generations of scholars had been more open to symbolic and allegorical interpretations of some of the biblical books.

Demythologizing

The German theologian Rudolf Bultmann (1884–1976) pioneered a new method of interpreting the Christian faith. He sought to demythologize the Gospels; this meant interpreting them rather than stripping the supernatural material away. This treated the supernatural as symbolic of

The importance of the New Testament mythology lies not in its imagery but in the understanding of existence which it enshrines.

RUDOLF BULTMANN,
THEOLOGY OF THE NEW TESTAMENT

BARTH AND NEO-ORTHODOXY

The German theologian Karl Barth (1886–1968) was a pastor in Geneva during the First World War, and his experiences there led him to rethink the theology he had been brought up with. He struggled with the New Testament writings, and especially those of Paul. He wrote *Der Romerbrief*, a commentary on Paul's epistle to the Romans, in 1919. This stressed that humanity was continually under God's judgment, and that his Word was addressed to us to challenge and to heal. God revealed his Word to us supremely in Jesus. Revelation was on the agenda again, and not just reason (i.e. what we could find out for ourselves). Barth held to a critical view of the scriptures, but, somehow, the Word of God is contained in and through these human words and traditions. When God speaks to us through them, the human words convey or become the Word of God. This position became known as neo-orthodoxy, and it inspired a generation of biblical scholars and theologians who could question this story or that miracle, but were orthodox in their understanding of Christ.

St Martin's Church and Cloth Hall ruins in Ypres, Belgium. The city of Ypres was almost totally destroyed during the First World War.

inner, existential states. The resurrection was our new life; the atonement was our reconciliation; the miracles were the joyful possibility of freedom of choice and new life here and now. He followed Heidegger's philosophy as a model. His view of miracles was typical of the Enlightenment age. He once stated that no one could believe in the New Testament view of the world any more.

The Postmodern Condition

'Postmodernism' is a term for a diverse movement, but there are some key ideas that signal the end of modernism.

Any movement that has the prefix 'post' is shifting beyond an earlier movement, reacting to it, but inseparably wedded to it. 'Postmodernism' means, literally, 'beyond the now', or 'beyond the modern'.

Let us wage war on totality…

JEAN-FRANÇOIS LYOTARD, THE POSTMODERN CONDITION

Rapid change

The end of the Second World War ushered in an era of reconstruction and technological growth. Change has become faster and faster, and information technology has revolutionized communication and society. TV and PCs, followed by the mobile phone and the Internet have created the world in the guise of a global village. Frederic Jameson, in

THE END OF THE GRAND NARRATIVE

A sense of irony and limitation was explored by Jean-François Lyotard (1925–99), who wrote his report on the state of scientific thinking in society, *The Postmodern Condition*, in 1979. He concluded that the age of the metanarrative was over. By this he meant an overarching scheme of how things hold together. This was true of Marxism, with its belief in inevitable social progress and emancipation, and of philosophy such as Hegel's, with its quest for the Absolute. This was also true of all religious systems, which sought to codify all existence and to provide dogmatic schemes. The Christian story, by which the Western world had lived for centuries, of creation, fall, redemption and an end to all things with the coming of the kingdom of God, was seen (at least in part) as a human construction, another scheme, the scaffolding of the imagination.

Lyotard waged war on all totalitarian systems of knowledge, seeing these as impossible and limiting.

Technological advancements have led to a rapidly changing, relativistic consumer society.

Postmodernism, or the Cultural Logic of Late Capitalism (1991), argues that the movement is a creature of its time, being thrown up by the fast-paced change of consumer society since 1950. Socio-economic conditions thus influence the thinking of the philosophers. In this milieu of rapid change, new information technology and multimedia share images and ideas around the world. Things seem to be in flux and all is relative. What anchors or values can be held onto in this void?

Irony and self-awareness

The term 'postmodernism' was first used by Charles Jenks in his book *The Language of Post-Modern Architecture* in 1975. He meant that there was a style that sought to deliberately mix those of different epochs in the same structure. This mingling and cross-referencing reveals a sense of irony, a self-awareness that we are part of the flow of time and history, and that each age has its style of art, building, fashion, thinking and so on. All our thoughts and creations are time-conditioned. Each era is of equal worth (though, by taste judgment, we may prefer one to another), and none is better just because it is fresher and newer, the latest craze in town. Postmodernism is ironically self-aware of the limits of human reason and our being in time.

Deconstructing Discourse

We are 'trapped' in the text of our language and discourse in one sense, but there are many different levels of meaning and possible interpretations.

Ludwig Wittgenstein broke ranks with the logical positivists, and opened up a new idea of language in his later writings. Here, he saw our words as social interactions, and humans practise a series of different language games in life. The rules that apply to rational, scientific discourse are different from those of the poetic and emotive, for example. This does not devalue the latter.

Ferdinand de Saussure's work involved a sense of free play and structured rules. We gave signs their meaning, but he saw an underlying set of rules that crossed cultures. He saw these rules as the deep structures of language. He called this semiotics, the study of signs. Central to his theory was binary opposition, the pairing of opposing concepts in thought, such as light and dark, hot and cold, good and evil. The anthropologist Claude Lévi-Strauss (1908–) built upon Saussure's ideas, and applied them to the study of tribal groups and culture in general. The deep structures of

POST-STRUCTURALISTS

A group of French philosophers followed a post-structuralist line. They questioned the rigidity and totality of the systems of Saussure and Lévi-Strauss. Michel Foucault (1926–84), for example, published a series of socio-historical studies of sexuality, crime and punishment, and madness. He was concerned to show that 'knowledge' is a power game, and that dominant groups and ideologies shape how we think. He spoke of 'archaeologies' of ideas, and by stripping them apart, and unveiling their history, they were demythologized. Meaning was a social contract.

binary opposition were embedded in culture, not just in our speech.

Derrida and deconstruction
The Algerian-born post-structuralist Jacques Derrida

(1930–) has moved the debate further forward. He has attacked the idea of a meta-language that can convey pure truth. We have to take the free play of signifiers seriously. Words are our creation. He

There is nothing outside the text.
JACQUES DERRIDA,
OF GRAMMATOLOGY

rejects what he calls logocentrism (from *logos*, 'reason'): the idea that reason and our words can correctly and totally convey reality. We live in discourse and we cannot step outside of human language to have a God's-eye view of things.

Derrida refutes 'a metaphysics of presence', whereby we can experience reality in the raw. All our thoughts and experiences are interpreted through the filter of language, and we cannot escape this. He also questions binary opposition. This is only one angle on things, and the second item is always inferior to the former. This need not always be the case – the dark can be peaceful and profound; cold can be welcomed as well as shunned.

Deconstruction is a tool to study philosophy as a text, and Derrida writes his own idiosyncratic commentaries on actual texts of other thinkers. He also looks for slippages in meaning, sudden interruptions or contradictory stances that he calls *aporia* – a path that is blocked, where no way can be found to make coherent sense. Thus, he looks for hidden meanings that may have been subconscious or influenced by the dominant culture: what might a text reveal, and what are the many possible meanings?

Woman

The 20th century saw the rise of feminism and new understandings of sexual difference. Postmodern reflections on this subject have opened up new ideas of the self and ethics.

In the ancient world, women were subordinate unless they had wealth and learning. Early Christianity seems to have had a more radical vision, with Jesus treating women as disciples and spending time talking with them, but the later church sanctioned patriarchy. Women were 'the weaker sex' and came under the headship of men. Women could find freedom to study and to express themselves in convents, but rarely elsewhere, unless they were of the higher nobility or royalty.

The Enlightenment began to question this, particularly on the continent, but the rational was usually associated with the masculine, and the irrational with the feminine. The 20th century saw increasing emancipation as women worked, studied at universities and had the right to vote. During the Second World War, many women replaced men in the workplace and on the farm; why should they rescind this when the men came home? Feminism grew in the 1960s, with increased affluence and access to higher education, as well as the sexual freedom that came with the contraceptive pill. Women struggled to define themselves, but this was usually in competition with men. They sought equality, or even superiority. Radical feminists saw all men as oppressors, and withdrew from their company as far as possible.

Made a woman?

A key issue is what is intrinsic to masculinity and femininity.

Luce Irigaray was dismissed from her teaching position at the École Freudienne at Vincennes in 1974 by her mentor Jacques Lacan for publishing her theories rejecting penis envy and his phallocentric theory.

LUCE IRIGARAY AND JULIA KRISTEVA

The French writer Luce Irigaray (1932–) attacks the whole patriarchal undergirding of Western philosophy. The elevation of reason/the *logos* (symbolized by the phallus) at the expense of the emotions and the body has repressed areas of life, and women in particular. Irigaray rejects Freud's idea of penis envy, whereby women sense an innate lack; women do not 'need' a penis, for their 'hole' is creative and mysterious, a dark continent of feeling and alternative insight.

Another French psychotherapist and writer, Julia Kristeva (1941–), explores the preverbal expression of infants, and the rhythms they establish with their mothers. She refers to this well of primal perception as the semiotic. This is the alter-ego of reason, and remains very much a part of us, even if sublimated by patri archal society.

These authors see gender difference as creative, for men and women act as 'the Other' to each other. There lies the ground of ethics, of responsibilities and of creative expression. We are not defined as solitary egos, but as beings in relation.

The nature/nurture debate presents us with alternatives. Perhaps men and women are fundamentally the same, but culture educates them to act differently. This teaches androgyny as an ideal. Difference is removed. Simone de Beauvoir stirred up this debate with *The Second Sex* in 1949.

> *One is not born, but rather becomes a woman.*
>
> SIMONE DE BEAUVOIR, *THE SECOND SEX*

Women working in a steel factory during the Second World War.

men and women. If women's bodies are designed differently to conceive and carry babies, it should hardly be surprising to find differences in their genes. The problem is what to make of these essential differences. This should not bar women from certain jobs, or from access to political power.

Postfeminism

Postfeminism seeks to embrace difference and not to erase it. It recognizes that there are intrinsic psychological and biological differences between

No Solid Ground?

Postmodern philosophy can appear to lead to a philosophical and ethical relativity; does postmodernism live in the land of 'Do As You Please'?

The natural sciences, that bedrock of rational reality that came from the Enlightenment, are not so solid any more. Quantum physics opened the doors of doubt. Albert Einstein (1879–1955) developed his theory of relativity, whereby time is not constant, but dependent upon velocity. Matter is also energy. Max Planck (1858–1947) spoke of the uncertainty and chaotic nature of subatomic physics. The movement of particles could not always be predicted. Atoms split apart into smaller and smaller units, and where might it end… if at all? Quarks are the most basic units known at present, so conceptual and miniscule that poetic, expressive language is used to describe them; they, apparently, possess 'natural or hidden beauty'! Matter is a dance of subatomic particles,

Albert Einstein.

and the chairs we sit upon are so much air and shifting atoms.

Werner Heisenberg opened up the question of the involvement of the observer in an experiment. His famous 'uncertainty principle' states that we cannot accurately know the position and the momentum of a particle simultaneously. This was a God's-eye view. Our perceptions (and their limitations) were involved in evaluating an experiment.

Who am I?

The postmodern self seems to be a clever fiction, a social construction formed by experiences and language. Thus declared the psychologist Jacques Lacan (1901–81), another of Freud's pupils. For him, self-consciousness grows with an elaborate building of symbols and images that come

> *I think where I am not, therefore*
> *I am where I do not think. Is what*
> *thinks in my place, then, another I?*
> JACQUES LACAN

from society. The 'self' is a sign! Who are we – id, superego or ego?

Critical caution

Some postmodern thinkers leave room for passionate belief and commitment to values and causes. Irigaray supports justice for women, the disabled and the elderly; Kristeva is involved in the French anti-racism organization SOS Racisme; Derrida does not reject the idea of meaning. Derrida tries to open a discourse up to see all the possible influences and levels of meaning at play. He rejects single, fixed meanings. Life is too complex for that, but there is purpose and meaning; he is not anti-rational, calling himself 'a man of the Enlightenment', but he teases us to see that reason alone is not all that we need to face life. These writers speak often of 'the Other' and our social responsibilities. Life is relational, and this is a sure ground for ethics. They dust off the old Golden Rule, 'Do unto others what you would have them do unto you.'

VIRTUAL REALITY?

Jean Baudrillard (1929–) is obsessed by images and virtual realities; consumer society manufactures them constantly for its own ends. Just what is real any more? He even asked if the Gulf War had ever really happened. Perhaps this was hyperbole, but we saw only the highlights that our media wanted us to see. It was the first media war with daily footage and briefings. Baudrillard might present a biting critique, but his only positive suggestion is to practise the art of philosophical seduction, teasing and questioning, and thus deliberately subverting power structures.

149

A Postmodern God?

What happens to faith in a postmodern society? If there are no fixed points or grand narratives, can religion survive?

The late 20th century did not witness a radical erosion of faith, but a blossoming in many and various ways. A spiritual thirst and quest was more and more acknowledged by people spiritual purpose too. Two responses to this quest have been the rise of the New Age movement, and what sociologists have called NRMs, 'new religious movements'.

Statue of Christ the Redeemer, Rio de Janeiro, Brazil.

outside the traditional faiths. Science and reason were not enough. The experience of the Second World War, ongoing struggles during the cold war and fear of nuclear weapons, as well as the pollution of the environment, led to a sense of betrayal by technology. We need ethical values and a

NRMs

NRMs are either new movements within an established faith, or sects that begin with a powerful individual. Take the Raelians, for example. They are primarily based in Canada, boasting about 55,000 members worldwide. Their founder,

Rael, a former French racing driver, claims that he met aliens who were the real gods of old.

Mystery

Beliefs are linked with intuitions and feelings, flashes of insight and the poetic imagination. The classical Christian tradition affirmed this when it spoke of God's mystery. Human words could only express so much about God, no matter how much was revealed to us. The mystics have always refused to speak of that which cannot be expressed. Paul counselled that we would be in the dark about some things this side of the grave: 'Now we see but a poor reflection; then we shall see face to face' (1 Corinthians 13:12).

Philosophers such as Derrida and Irigaray seem to be fascinated by religious thought. Kristeva is an atheist, but she sees religious symbols as extremely valuable, and she speaks of the power of love as though it is almost a mystical force. Their questionings have reopened philosophy up to the expressive. Lyotard, too, admitted the need for the sublime and the abstract, best expressed in avant-garde poetry and art.

Perhaps we cannot get out of our skins and use other than human language, maybe metanarratives are partly human creations, but we can seek to express, however imperfectly, the divine. 'Revelation' must come in our words, and it is best understood as a cooperative dance between God and humanity. Our ideas can be ways of seeing beyond. Christianity is based upon the belief that the Word of God became flesh; in a flesh-and-blood man we see the divine most clearly, in our skin.

> *Let us be witnesses to the unpresentable.*
>
> JEAN-FRANÇOIS LYOTARD,
> *THE POSTMODERN CONDITION*

Summing up

The fast-paced inventions of modernity provoked an intellectual crisis, whereby the rational was questioned. Modernism gave way to postmodernism with even greater change, and there were no longer any fixed points. Human discourse and experience are open, suggestive, playful and relational.

'O, Man, Where are You?'

Our ideas can be healing, helpful or destructive. We have the ability to inspire and to enslave. Our freedom to act is indeed a terrible thing, and faith must be seen in the light of this.

Philosophers have speculated whether God is a human invention or not. Freud and Marx thought that he was a projection of our deepest hopes and wishes. If he is just an idea, then it is an amazing idea. That human beings in one corner of the universe, in a brief slice of the ages of time, could have come into being to think up such lofty thoughts is incredible. Ancient thinkers would have seen a proof of God's reality in this, in the ontological argument, for how could imperfect, fallible beings conceive of the Supreme, the Sublime, the Perfect? Perhaps the idea is not an illusion, but a hint of a Presence.

What we ultimately believe about God depends upon our view of life, our philosophy of things. A common cry against belief is a protest about all the pain and suffering in the world. How could God allow this to happen?

A rabbi was once asked this question by an interviewer. He had survived the death-camp,

> *Because he [God] may*
> *well be loved, but not thought.*
> *By love he can be caught and*
> *held, but by thinking never.*
>
> THE CLOUD OF UNKNOWING,
> 14TH CENTURY

Noli me tangere
by Fra Angelico
(1387–1455) in
San Marco,
Florence.

Auschwitz. He rounded upon the interviewer, telling her that she was asking the wrong question: 'You should be asking, "Where was man when all those things were happening?"'

He recounted how, on one Day of Atonement in the Jewish calendar, he had sneaked behind one of the bunkers to say the traditional prayers. He felt a presence with him, an infinitely sad presence, and he began to weep. This was God grieving for all the horrible acts that his creation had perpetrated. It seemed to well up within him and around him. God was weeping down the ages. Where was humanity? How could *Homo sapiens*, with all their reason and wisdom, have acted worse than brute beasts?

The history of ideas must take stock of the corruption and flawed nature of humanity;

> *Do not hold on to me, for I have*
> *not yet returned to the Father.*
>
> JESUS, JOHN 20:17

we can aspire to be gods, but we can also stoop low enough to act like demons.

Untouchable

Faith is beyond reason, but not wholly irrational. It is not a blind leap in the dark, for reasonable grounds for belief can be brought forward. A good way to conclude is to consider Fra Angelico's painting of the risen Christ appearing to Mary Magdalene. *Noli me tangere (Do Not Touch Me)* shows Christ walking ahead, his hand stretched out towards Mary, but just in front of her, not connected. He moves, not quite in touch with the ground, calling her forth, drawing her on. This is a representation of the mystery of God, calling us to walk by faith in the face of puzzle, paradox, mystery and awe. God is a reality always ahead of us, beyond us, undecipherable and exterior to analysis. We could be just a chance product of chemicals mixing together and evolving, or we could be in the centre of immensities. It is up to us to decide.

Rapid Factfinder

A

anamnesis: 'remembrance'; used by Plato for the idea of recalling knowledge of the world of ideals when we are born into the world. We learn by remembering what we once knew.

anatman: the Buddhist idea that there is nothing permanent in us, no immortal soul.

arche: the foundation, the basis of all things, the basic 'stuff' from which the universe is made.

archetypes: Carl Jung's term for universal images and symbols that are carried in humanity's psyche, such as 'the shadow' or the wise philosopher.

atman: Hindu concept of the spark of divine life within a person, the 'soul'.

B

bhakti: the Hindu way of devotion to a personal deity.

Brahman: the name for ultimate reality in the Hindu Upanishads.

Buddha: 'Enlightened One', supremely seen in the life of Siddhartha Gautama.

C

Cartesian dualism: the supposed radical separation of body and soul in Descartes' thought – a 'ghost in the machine'. In fact, Descartes believed that the two substances were profoundly united.

chun-tzu: the Confucian idea of the nobleman. A true nobleman is not one by birth, but by inner attitude and virtue.

clear and distinct ideas: Descartes' notion that only things the mind can perceive as simple realities are to be trusted as being real.

cogito: the thinking subject, according to Descartes.

cosmological argument: Aquinas's idea that the existence of the world pointed to the existence of a creator.

D

deconstruction: Derrida's attempt to tease out the many influences at play in a text, both conscious and unconscious.

demythologizing: Rudolf Bultmann's idea that supernatural events in the Gospels could be reinterpreted in terms of existential theology. A miracle was totally interior, a new insight or beginning experienced by a person.

Dreamtime: Aborigine idea of a mythical time before the world was created.

dying/rising gods: fertility deities symbolizing the renewing power of nature, such as Osiris or Balder.

E

ego: the rational, conscious mind.

empiricism: the idea that only our five senses can be trusted to determine what is true.

Encyclopédie: the collection of knowledge about different topics by Diderot and D'Alembert in a series of 28 volumes, published in the 18th century.

Enlightenment: the Age of Reason in shaping the modern world, forming the scientific method and critical ways of observing reality.

exodus: the escape of the Hebrew slaves from slavery in Egypt, when led by Moses.

F

First Cause: The principle that begins all other things, the cause of motion and all change, the origin of the universe. The irony is that a First Cause needs to be outside space/time as the latter is caused by it.

four noble truths: the key Buddhist teaching on the nature of life. Life is impermanent, and suffering is all around, but there is a path that leads to release.

fundamentalism: a movement that began by affirming key areas of Christian doctrine, but came to mean a literal understanding of the Bible.

H

Hadith: traditions about the Prophet Muhammad not contained in the Qur'an.

I

id: the unconscious mind, full of passions and drives, according to Freud.

ideal forms: Plato's idea that behind each object in the changing, varied world, there is an ideal form – all chairs partake in the ideal form of 'chairness'.

Islam: 'submission' to the will of God; a Muslim is 'one who submits'.

J

jihad: Arabic term meaning 'struggle', spiritual or physical.

K

karma: the Hindu idea of the record of good and bad deeds that determines your fate in this life and the next.

khalifa: Arabic term meaning that human beings are God's deputies, his stewards on earth.

L

logical positivism: early 20th-century analysis of language, which stated that meaning was only in what was logical; emotional speech was nonsense, and anything that was beyond sense experience was rejected, such as religious beliefs.

M

maya: the Indian idea of the world as 'illusion', meaning a temporary reality that is always changing.

Messiah: 'anointed one', the promised king of the Jews.

metanarratives: 'grand narratives' about philosophy, religion, science or politics.

modernism: the philosophical and aesthetic movement in the early 20th century that celebrated rapid change, and sought to rediscover mystery and the emotions in avant-garde literature and art.

modernity: the late 19th and early 20th centuries, with their inventions and rapid social change.

moksha: 'release' or 'liberty'. One escapes from being endlessly reincarnated to join God.

monophysites: 'one nature'; a group of Christians who believed that Jesus was one being as God and man, a real unity, and not two parallel substances that did not unite.

mystery cults: secret religious societies in the Greco-Roman world that initiated people into the spiritual mysteries of dying and rising gods.

myth: a symbolic story that might try to explain why things are the way they are in picturesque, fantastical ways. Myths can contain deep insights about human values, hopes and fears.

N

natural selection: Charles Darwin's mechanism to explain how evolution works; the survival of the fittest.

neo-orthodoxy: a movement begun by Karl Barth in the early 20th century that embraced biblical criticism, but retained an orthodox Christian faith.

nirvana: the Buddhist idea of being cooled from all passions and finding bliss and peace.

O

ontological argument: Anselm's idea that the concept of God is so perfect and beyond human imagination that God must therefore exist in reality.

P

Pax Romana: the 'Roman peace'; the period of peace and stability in the Roman empire from the start of the emperor Augustus's reign (31 BCE) for over 200 years.

philosophes: French thinkers who frequented coffee houses and salons in Paris in the 18th century.

postfeminism: a movement that reacted to certain forms of feminism by seeking to affirm the difference between the sexes as well as their equality.

postmodernism: moving beyond modernism to an era where we expect constant fads and fashions in style and ideology. It is critical, cynical and ironic, but can lead to a rediscovery of mystery, symbols and transcendence.

post-structuralism: a movement that repudiates structuralist analysis, and celebrates mystery and the inexpressible.

pre-Socratics: the Greek philosophers who came before Socrates, such as Thales, Pythagoras and Heraclitus.

psychoanalysis: a method of studying the dreams, speech and mannerisms of a patient to shed light upon their emotional state – pioneered by Sigmund Freud.

Q

Qur'an: the holy book of Islam, meaning 'that which was recited'.

R

reductionism: the idea that an object or an action can be conceptually broken down into smaller parts, in order to understand it.

Renaissance: the 'rebirth' of learning in 13th and 14th-century Europe.

S

shamans: tribal holy men and medicine men who believed that they could mediate with the gods.

sharia: 'the way', according to Islam. A collection of written and oral traditions that includes laws.

structuralism: an early 20th-century movement that sought to analyse language and symbols according to strict rules and formulas. There were 'deep structures' beneath everyday speech and folk customs.

Sunna: the whole tradition of Islam – Qur'an, Hadith, oral traditions and the consensus of the community.

superego: Freud's idea that the unconscious mind has a filter or a censor to stop certain things getting through to the ego.

T

tabula rasa: Locke's idea that the human mind is a 'blank slate' at birth. Experiences and physical interactions create the conscious mind and memory.

Tao: the path or way, understood as an impersonal but vital force that flows through all living things in Chinese thought.

teleological argument: Aquinas's argument that everything has its *telos*, or purpose. Things are designed to work in a certain way, and this points to a creator, as does the question of what the *telos* of the whole cosmos is. There must be a transcendent purpose.

teleology: Aristotle's idea that each created thing had an innate purpose, so fire existed to burn, a knife to cut and so on.

Torah: the 'Way' or 'Law' of Moses, being the first five books of the Hebrew Bible.

W

Wu-wei: a Taoist term for not resisting – for following the *Tao* or 'going with the flow'.

Index of Key Thinkers

Augustine of Hippo (354–430 CE): African bishop and theologian who expressed insights about the Christian faith in the terms of Greek philosophy.

Anselm of Canterbury (1033–1109 CE): archbishop and theologian who originated the ontological argument to 'prove' God's existence.

Thomas Aquinas (c. 1225–74): Italian Dominican friar who integrated the works of Aristotle into Christian theology.

Aristotle (384–322 BCE): Greek philosopher who wrote about many subjects. He thought that everything had its own *telos*, or purpose, for which it was made.

Marcus Aurelius (121–80 CE): Roman emperor and Stoic philosopher who sought to follow the *logos* reflected in his own reason and conscience.

Francis Bacon (1561–1626): Lord Chancellor in Elizabethan England and philosopher. He divided knowledge into three areas (memory, imagination and reason), dealing with the areas of history, the arts, philosophy and the sciences.

Karl Barth (1886–1968): Swiss theologian who encouraged neo-orthodoxy, affirming basic Christian doctrine in his many-volumed *Church Dogmatics*.

Jean Baudrillard (1929–): French postmodern philosopher who is concerned with reality, the media and illusion.

Rudolf Bultmann (1884–1976): German theologian who pioneered demythologizing.

Confucius (551–479 BCE): Chinese official and philosopher who taught social justice and respect through ethical codes.

Charles Darwin (1809–82): scientist and creator of the theory of evolution by natural selection.

Jacques Derrida (1930–): Algerian-born, post-structuralist philosopher working in Paris. He pioneered deconstruction.

René Descartes (1596–1650): French philosopher who questioned the Scholastics and the foundations of medieval thought. He trusted only the *cogito* – the thinking self – and the clear and distinct ideas it could form about the external world.

Denis Diderot (1713–84): French philosopher and compiler of the *Encyclopédie*.

Sigmund Freud (1856–1939): Austrian doctor who pioneered psychoanalysis and the interpretation of dreams.

Georg Wilhelm Friedrich Hegel (1770–1831): German philosopher who developed dialectics, whereby a thesis and antithesis becomes a synthesis. He also believed that *Geist*, or Spirit, guided history and was leading humanity to a knowledge of the absolute.

Martin Heidegger (1889–1976): German philosopher, and a pupil of Husserl. He developed phenomenology into what became known as existentialism.

Heraclitus (c. 540–480 BCE): pre-Socratic philosopher who taught that everything was in constant flux.

David Hume (1711–76): Scottish philosopher who worked during the Enlightenment. He was sceptical about supernatural and religious claims, but also chided empiricists for basing so much on observation alone.

Edmund Husserl (1859–1938): German philosopher who taught phenomenology, and thought that only our experiences were a direct knowledge of reality.

Carl Gustav Jung (1875–1961): A disciple of Freud who deviated sharply from his ideas, developing his own methods of psycho-analysis. He taught that there was a collective unconscious, and that certain symbols were potent and universal.

Immanuel Kant (1724–1804): German philosopher who wrote about ethics and knowledge. He saw sense experience as a filter, a means of interpreting external reality, rather than a totally accurate representation of it.

Søren Kierkegaard (1813–55): Danish philosopher who struggled with the relationship between faith and reason, teaching an early form of existentialism.

Jacques Lacan (1901–81): French psychotherapist who developed Freud's ideas, seeing language as formative for human consciousness and self-image.

Lao Tzu (6th century BCE): Chinese sage and philosopher who taught the *Tao* and was said to be the author of the *Tao Te Ching*.

Claude Lévi-Strauss (1908–): structural anthropologist who applied structuralist analysis to human societies.

John Locke (1632–1704): English philosopher in the early Enlightenment who taught empiricism. He trusted only what the five senses told us about the external world.

Jean-François Lyotard (1925–99): French postmodern philosopher who argued that metanarratives were now impossible, as each age is culturally conditioned in its ideas.

Karl Marx (1818–83): German émigré who lived and wrote in London, developing ideas of class struggle and history that formed communism.

Isaac Newton (1642–1727): English scientist who proposed laws of motion and gravity.

Friedrich Nietzsche (1844–1900): German philosopher who questioned many received traditions and attitudes, trying to subvert morality and the idea of 'truth'.

Plato (427–347 BCE): Greek philosopher and a disciple of Socrates. He wrote down his master's teachings, and developed his own ideas about the perfect world of ideals and the imperfect, changing world we live in.

Pythagoras (c. 580–500 BCE): pre-Socratic philosopher and mystic who formed communities and taught that numbers were mystical.

Jean-Jacques Rousseau (1712–78): French Enlightenment thinker who moved away from a stress on reason to the emotions. He taught that primitive societies were more natural and free.

Bertrand Russell (1872–1970): English philosopher who followed a version of logical positivism known as logical atomism, breaking sentences down into their logical component parts. Again, only what was empirical was reasonable.

Jean-Paul Sartre (1905–80): French existentialist philosopher who taught that life offered a terrifying freedom to 'be' in the face of nothingness.

Socrates (470–399 BCE): Greek philosopher who was famous for holding dialogues rather than writing anything down. An honest seeker after truth, a radical thinker who challenged convention and trusted reason and conscience.

Baruch Spinoza (1632–77): Dutch-Jewish philosopher who argued that there was one substance to reality, that of God, and that soul and body were different modes or aspects of this being.

Paul Tillich (1886–1965): German theologian who later settled in the USA. He argued that images of depth were more useful than those of height when speaking about God, declaring God to be 'the Ground of our Being'.

Voltaire (1694–1778): French rationalist and novelist who attacked the old order and sought a fairer society.

Ludwig Wittgenstein (1889–1951): Austrian philosopher who settled in Cambridge, England, and began as a logical positivist, but broke away from these confines later. He taught that language used a variety of 'games' to cover different types of expression.

Picture
Acknowledgments

AKG Berlin: pp. 2 (left), 2 (right), 5, 7, 17, 24–25, 28, 32–33, 36–37, 38, 40, 42–43, 46, 48–49, 53, 58–59, 61, 62, 67, 68, 69, 71, 74, 75, 88–89, 100, 111, 120, 126, 127, 134–35, 137, 138, 152–53.

Ann Ronan Picture Library: cover, pp. 18, 20–21, 22–23, 32, 34, 45, 65, 77, 83, 84, 86, 90, 92, 96–97, 98–99, 101, 103, 104, 105, 108, 112–13, 114–15, 117, 118, 119, 121, 122–23, 125, 128–29, 132, 136, 139.

Art Directors and Trip: pp. 12 (R. Nichols), 13 (A. Kuznetsov), 70 (A. Tovy), 87, 94–95, 85 (K. Maclaren), 106–107 (T. Why).

Corbis: pp. 3 (Burstein Collection [right]), 54 (Burstein Collection), 73 (Archivo Iconografico, S.A.), 140–41 (Hulton-Deutsch Collection).

Digital Vision: pp. 3 (left), 6, 11, 16, 19, 56, 110–11, 142–43, 150–51.

Gamma: pp. 4 (Alan Chin), 8–9 (Ministere de la Culture/Lyo Drac), 21, 80–81, 90–91 (Alan Chin), 95 (Gilles Bassignac), 145 (Ducasse Christian).

Heritage-Images: pp. 72 (British Museum), 93 (British Museum).

ImageState: pp. 14–15, 26–27, 30–31, 54–55.

Topfoto: pp. 130 (UPPA).

Topham: pp. 50 (AP), 79 (ImageWorks), 131 (UPPA), 135, 148 (Photri), 149 (UNEP).

TophamPicturepoint: pp. 109, 146–47, 147.